THE 100+ SERIES™

Reproducible Activities

Using the Standards

Number & Operations

Grade 5

By

Becky Daniel

Published by Instructional Fair
an imprint of
Frank Schaffer Publications®

Instructional Fair

Author: Becky Daniel
Editor: Rebecca Warren

Frank Schaffer Publications®

Instructional Fair is an imprint of Frank Schaffer Publications.

Send all inquiries to:
Frank Schaffer Publications
3195 Wilson Drive NW
Grand Rapids, Michigan 49534

Using the Standards: Numbers & Operations—grade 5

ISBN: 0-7424-1815-4

4 5 6 7 8 9 10 PAT 10 09 08 07 06 05

Table of Contents

Published by Instructional Fair. Copyright protected.

0-7424-1815-4 *Numbers & Operations*

Introduction

By the fifth grade, students should have a firm grasp on number systems—the way numbers are represented and how they relate to each other. The first chapter, **Number Systems,** provides practice in understanding numbers and contains activities to introduce, teach, and reinforce:

- negative numbers
- place-value structure of the base-ten number system
- decimals
- equivalent representations of numbers (can decompose and compose numbers)
- models to use in judging size and making comparisons
- equivalent forms of commonly used fractions, decimals, and percents
- finding least common denominators, multiples, and greatest common factors

The second chapter, **Operations**, explores the meaning of adding, subtracting, multiplying, and dividing as individual operations as well as connections between the operations. The highly motivating worksheets will provide practice in:

- whole numbers and the relationships between them (addition as repeated multiplication and division as the inverse of multiplication)
- commutative property and distributive property
- choosing from the four operations (addition, subtraction, multiplication, division) to solve word problems

The last chapter, **Computation**, will help students develop and use strategies for computations such as rounding off, creating models, and mental computations. The activities were carefully designed to give students practice in number computation and opportunities to make reasonable estimations. The worksheets in this chapter will provide students opportunities to develop:

- fluency with multiplication and division facts
- fluency in adding, subtracting, multiplying, and dividing whole numbers
- computation skills involving fractions, decimals, percents, and ratio
- ability to compute whole numbers with mental computation, estimation, calculators, and paper and pencil exercises

For easy record keeping, a Check Your Skills page is provided at the end of each chapter. Compiled, the three-page skills checklists will provide you with a comprehensive mathematical continuum for individualized records. For easy access, a file folder containing each student's pretest (pages 7–8), skill check pages (pages 53, 76, and 108), and post test (pages 109–110) can make record keeping quick and easy.

The 100+ activity sheets herein were developed in accordance with standards as prescribed by the National Council for Teachers of Mathematics. Each of the three chapters—Number Systems, Operations,

4

and Computation—is based on one of the three major content strands for Number and Operations. Each chapter contains a sampling of the five process strands for mathematics:

- Problem Solving
- Reasoning and Proof
- Communication
- Connections
- Representation

Look for the icons at the top of each page to see which process strands are covered by that page. Or check the Correlation to NCTM Standards chart on page 6 for a listing of page numbers by process strand.

Problem solving is the foundation for all other mathematics. The ability to solve problems makes mathematics a life skill needed by all students for success in the adult world. Everyday situations such as buying food, planning party recipes, or surveying friends to find out their favorites are all problem-centered approaches that will motivate even your most reluctant students.

Reasoning and proof are fundamental aspects of mathematics that require the learner to make assumptions and to investigate whether an idea is sound. Estimating the sum, difference, product, or quotient before actually calculating makes it possible for students to verify their work as they progress.

Language is as important to solving math problems as it is when learning to read. In order to make assumptions and test ideas, students must be able to clearly **communicate** their thoughts. In the classroom, provide opportunities for students to meet in pairs or small groups to discuss the methods they used to solve the problems. Encourage students to demonstrate a variety of methods for solving story problems.

When students learn to make assumptions, test their assumptions, and can discuss them coherently, they will be able to recognize and use **connections** among mathematical ideas. For example, if students see pies cut into fourths, sixths, eighths, and tenths, then finding the differences of unlike fractions should be a piece of cake, or should I say, as easy as pie?

As students begin to recognize multiple **representations** of numbers, they will be able to organize, record, look for patterns, and communicate mathematical ideas. This will enable them to solve problems in multiple ways.

When students are taught to problem solve, reason to prove, communicate mathematical ideas, make connections, and use representation to interpret mathematical phenomena, math will become more than numbers and operations. Mathematics will become the key to understanding our universe and how everything in it relates to everything else.

5

 0-7424-1815-4 *Numbers & Operations*

Correlation to NCTM Standards

	Problem Solving	Reasoning and Proof	Communication	Connections	Representation
Number Systems	10, 13, 18, 20, 26, 28, 30, 48, 50, 51	12, 16, 19, 20, 24, 25, 28, 33, 47	14, 21, 22, 23, 29, 38, 43, 44, 46, 47	9, 10, 11, 12, 13, 14, 15, 17, 18, 19, 24, 25, 27, 29, 31, 32, 36, 37, 38, 39, 40, 41, 42, 45, 46, 48, 49, 52	9, 15, 16, 17, 21, 22, 23, 26, 33, 34, 35, 36, 37, 39, 40, 41, 42, 43, 44, 45
Operations	58, 59, 60, 65, 66, 67, 68, 72, 73, 74, 75	57, 64, 70	54, 55, 63, 67	54, 55, 56, 57, 58, 61, 62, 63, 65, 68, 69, 70, 71, 72, 73, 74, 75	59, 60, 61, 62, 64
Computation	78, 79, 80, 86, 94, 95, 96, 97, 99, 100, 101, 102, 103, 106, 107	81, 82, 83, 84, 85, 87, 88, 95, 98	77, 82, 87, 88, 89, 96, 107	77, 80, 86, 90, 91, 92, 93, 94, 100, 101, 102, 103, 104, 105, 106	81, 83, 84, 85, 89, 92, 97, 98, 99

Pretest

1. What is the absolute value of $^-7$? _____

2. Write nine million, seven hundred thousand, ninety-two. _____

3. Round 8,678,234 to the nearest hundred thousand. _____

4. **a.** Write 9,901,450 in expanded form.

   _____

   b. What is the value of the 1? _____

5. In 85.297, which numeral represents hundredths? _____

6. **a.** Shade $\frac{3}{10}$ of the bar.

   b. What fractional part of the bar is not shaded? _____

7. Complete the chart.

Decimal	Fraction	Percent
0.5		
	$\frac{1}{100}$	

8. What is the least common denominator of $\frac{1}{3}$ and $\frac{5}{8}$? _____

9. What is the least common multiple of 4 and 12? _____

10. What is the greatest common factor of 11 and 33? _____

11. The commutative property of addition means that changing the _____ of the addends does not change the sum.

12. The associative property of addition means that changing the way _____ are grouped does not change the sum.

7

Published by Instructional Fair. Copyright protected.

Pretest

13. In 5 x 6 = 30, 30 is the _____ and 5 and 6 are the _____.

14. Write this equation as a multiplication problem: 5 + 5 + 5 + 5 + 5 + 5 = _____

15. Write an addition, multiplication, and division equation for this figure:

_____   _____

_____

16. If 10 hens can lay 60 eggs per week, how long will it take 100 hens to lay 600 eggs?
_____

17. If a cookie recipe calls for $\frac{2}{3}$ cup sugar, how much sugar will you need to make 6 batches of cookies? _____

18. 19.23 + 12.9 =

19. 744.06 – 0.566 =

20. $\frac{7}{12} + \frac{9}{12} =$

21. $\frac{1}{4} - \frac{1}{8} =$

22. $\frac{1}{3} \times \frac{3}{8} =$

23. $\frac{1}{3} \div \frac{1}{2} =$

24. ⁻16 + ⁻1 =

25. ⁻2 x ⁻864 =

26. ⁻1,586 + 13 =

27. If Mrs. Jericho wants to make 9 pizzas for her bridge club, and 1 pizza calls for $\frac{3}{4}$ pounds of cheese, how many pounds of cheese will she need? _____

28. **a.** If $\frac{1}{6}$ of the circle is yellow, how many sections are yellow? _____

b. If $\frac{1}{3}$ of the circle is green, how many sections are not green? _____

0-7424-1815-4 *Numbers & Operations*

Name _____ Date _____

Name That Value

millions	hundred thousands	ten thousands	thousands	hundreds	tens	ones
8,	1	2	3,	0	4	9

Directions: Write your answers to show the place value of the given digit in the number above. Use an equation to show the place value. The first one has been done for you.

1. What is the value of the 4? _____ 4 x 10 = 40 _____

2. What is the value of the 8? _____

3. What is the value of the 2? _____

4. What is the value of the 3? _____

5. What place is represented by the 0? _____

6. What place is represented by the 1? _____

7. How many millions are there? _____

8. How many tens are there? _____

9. What is the value of the 9? _____

10. What is the value of the 1? _____

Do More: In a number 3 times as large as 8,123,049, what numeral represents hundred thousands? Take a guess. Then use a calculator to find out.

9

Name _____ Date _____

Big Winners

Place value is determined by the position of a digit in a number.

Example: In 5,678, the place value of 5 is 5,000,000, or five million.

Millions Period	Thousands Period	Hundreds Period
hundred million	hundred thousand	hundred
ten million	ten thousand	ten
one million	one thousand	one

Directions: Pretend that you and your 2 best friends won the lotto. The prize is $11,240,955.30 Use the lotto winnings to solve each word problem. Show your work.

1. Who are your 2 best friends? _____ and _____

2. Of the total winnings, what is the place value of the:
    a. 2? _____
    b. 4? _____
    c. 9? _____

3. There are 3 of you in total who will share the winnings. How much will you each get?
    _____

4. In your share of the winnings, what digit is in the:
    a. hundreds place? _____
    b. ones place? _____
    c. ten thousands place? _____

5. In your share of the winnings, what place value is the:
    a. 7? _____
    b. 3? _____
    c. 8? _____

6. If you decide to give $700,000 to your parents to put in a savings account for you, how much will you have left? _____

7. If both of your friends decide to donate half of their money to charity, what would be the sum of their contributions? _____

8. Write out the total winnings in word form.
    _____

Name _____ Date _____

Searching for Sevens

Directions: Look at the numbers inside the design. Each number contains one numeral 7. Color each section according to the place value held by the seven.

ones = blue	ten thousands = green
tens = orange	hundred thousands = red
hundreds = yellow	millions = white
thousands = purple	

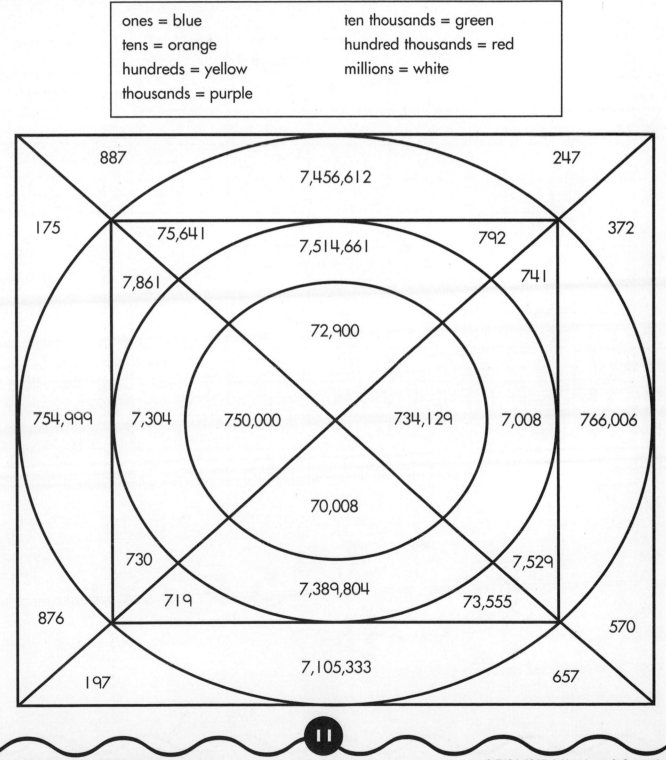

0-7424-1815-4 *Numbers & Operations*

Name _____ Date _____

The Value's Right On

Directions: Complete this chart by writing a number represented by each row of digits. The first one has been done for you.

	ones	tens	hundreds	thousands	ten thousands	hundred thousands		number
1.	1				4	5	=	540,001
2.		5	7		3	8	=	
3.		5	6	9			=	
4.	9	5		7	1	3	=	
5.	6		8		2	2	=	
6.		7	5	5	3	8	=	
7.	2	9	1	6	4	3	=	
8.	2	5	7	2	9	5	=	
9.	7	6	2	4		1	=	
10.	8	4		6		5	=	
11.	9	5	7	8	1	4	=	
12.	2	4	7	9	2	3	=	

0-7424-1815-4 *Numbers & Operations*

Name _____ Date _____

Rounding Off at the Roundup

If the digit is less than 5, **round down**. If the digit is 5 or greater, **round up**.	Example: 43 rounds down to 40 45 rounds up to 50 47 round up to 50

Directions: Slim Jim owns the Bar None Ranch, the biggest cattle ranch in Texas. At roundup, Slim and his team counted 1,043,512 steer.

1. Round off the number of steer to the nearest ten thousand. _____

2. If rounded off to the nearest million, how many steer would Slim say that he owned?

   _____

3. If rounded off to the nearest thousand, how many steer would Slim say that he owned?

   _____

4. If rounded off to the nearest million, how many steer would be left out of the count? _____

5. At which place value will the number be rounded up instead of down? _____

6. If rounded off to the nearest thousand, what digit will be a double digit in the figure? _____

7. If Slim can transport 10 steer in a moving truck, and it costs $100 for a truck and driver to get the steer to the marketplace, how much will it cost to move 1,000,000 head of cattle?

   _____

8. If a head of steer goes for $120 at market, approximately how much money will Slim get for his herd? Round off the number of steer to the nearest million to make your estimate.

   _____

13

 0-7424-1815-4 *Numbers & Operations*

Name _____ Date _____

Most Populated States

> **Short word form** means that a number is written using both numerals and words.
> Example: 3,533 = 3 thousand, 5 hundred, 33

Most Populated States

Most Populated States	
California	31,589,153
Texas	18,723,991
New York	18,136,081
Pennsylvania	12,071,842

Directions: Write the population of each state in short word form. The first one has been done for you. Then round off the populations as directed.

1. California   <u>31 million, 589 thousand, 1 hundred, 53</u>

2. Texas   _____

3. New York   _____

4. Pennsylvania _____

5. Round off California to the nearest thousand.   <u>31,589,000</u>

6. Round off Texas to the nearest million.   _____

7. Round off New York to the nearest million.   _____

8. Round off Pennsylvania to the nearest thousand. _____

Do More: The total number of people in the United States is always growing. Estimate the U.S. population today. To check your estimation and find out the population of United States, go to the U.S. Census Bureau Population Clocks at `http://www.census.gov/main/www/popclock`.

   0-7424-1815-4 *Numbers & Operations*

Name _____ Date _____

By Any Other Name

What do your friends call you? Do you have a nickname? What do your parents call you? Just as you may have more than one name, there are many names for the same number.

Standard form is a way of writing a number using numerals.
   Example: 12,345

Expanded form is a way of writing a number as the sum of the values of its digits.
   Example: 12,345 = 10,000 + 2,000 + 300 + 40 + 5

Word form is a way of writing a number using only words.
   Example: 12,345 = twelve thousand three hundred forty-five

Short word form means that a number is written using both numerals and words.
   Example: 12,345 = 12 thousand, 3 hundred, 45

Directions: Answer the questions below using what you know about number names.

1. Write the number 1,360 three different ways.
   a. _____
   b. _____
   c. _____

2. Write the number 56,781 three different ways.
   a. _____
   b. _____
   c. _____

3. How many different ways can you think of to name the number 36?
   _____
   _____

4. Write each number that is being described.
   a. This number is the opposite of $^+6$. _____
   b. This integer is negative and has an absolute value of $^+5$. _____
   c. 8,000 + 900 + 50 + 3 is the same as _____
   d. 999 + 1 = _____
   e. five hundred sixty-nine and one half _____
   f. 5 million, 600 thousand, 5 hundred 43 _____

Do More: Write your address in expanded form.

0-7424-1815-4 *Numbers & Operations*

Name _____ Date _____

Representational Form

Representational form is a way of writing a number using base-ten blocks:
Example: 2,345   **expanded form:** 2,000 + 300 + 40 + 5
word form: two thousand three hundred forty-five
representational form:

Directions: Fill in the missing portion of each problem below with the correct form.

1. standard form: _____   expanded form: _____
   word form: _____   representational form:
   _____

2. standard form: _____   expanded form: 700 + 80 + 5
   word form: _____   representational form:
   _____

3. standard form: 5,010 _____   expanded form: _____
   word form: _____   representational form:
   _____

4. standard form: _____   expanded form: _____
   word form: eight thousand seventy-two   representational form:
   _____

5. standard form: _____   expanded form: 10,000 + 2,000 + 10 + 1
   word form: _____   representational form:
   _____

0-7424-1815-4 *Numbers & Operations*

Name _____ Date _____

The Same Number

Directions: Complete the number chart by writing each number three ways.

```
Example: 186
        expanded form: 100 + 80 + 6
        short word form: 1 hundred, 86
        word form: one hundred eighty-six
```

1. 3,940

    expanded form: _____

    short word form: _____

    word form: _____

    _____

2. 1,122

    expanded form: _____

    short word form: _____

    word form: _____

    _____

3. 1,960

    expanded form: _____

    short word form: _____

    word form: _____

    _____

4. 4,789,456

    expanded form: _____

    short word form: _____

    word form: _____

Do More: Estimate how many days old you are. Use a calculator to find out. Don't forget to adjust for leap years.

0-7424-1815-4 *Numbers & Operations*

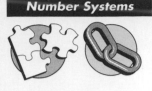

Name _____ Date _____

What's Next?

Directions: Look at each group of numbers. Fill in the blanks after you have determined the missing numbers. Then answer the questions about each group of numbers.

1. 67,809; _____; 67,811; _____; _____
    a. How many hundreds? _____
    b. How many thousands? _____
    c. How many ten thousands? _____

2. _____; 7,002; _____; _____; 7,005
    a. Write the fourth number in this series in expanded form.
    _____

    b. Write the third number in this series in word form.
    _____

    c. On the back of this page, show the first number in this series in representational form.

3. 5,001,302; _____; _____; 5,001,305; _____
    a. How many millions? _____
    b. How many thousands? _____
    c. How many hundred thousands? _____

4. 11,010; _____; _____; _____; 11,014
    a. Write the second number in this series in expanded form.
    _____

    b. Write the third number in this series in word form.
    _____

    c. Show the fourth number in this series in representational form.

5. 1,998; _____; _____; 2,001; _____
    a. How many ones in the second number? _____
    b. How many thousands in the first number? _____
    c. How many thousands in the last number? _____

Do More: Make a number line and include all the numbers on this page.

18

Name _____ Date _____

Number Charts

In a number chart, when the numbers go **across**, the numbers change by **1**.
When the numbers go **up or down**, the numbers change by **10**.

15	16	17
25		
35		

+10 ↕

+1 ↔

Directions: Write the numbers 1 through 100 in the chart. Use the information to fill in the partial charts below.

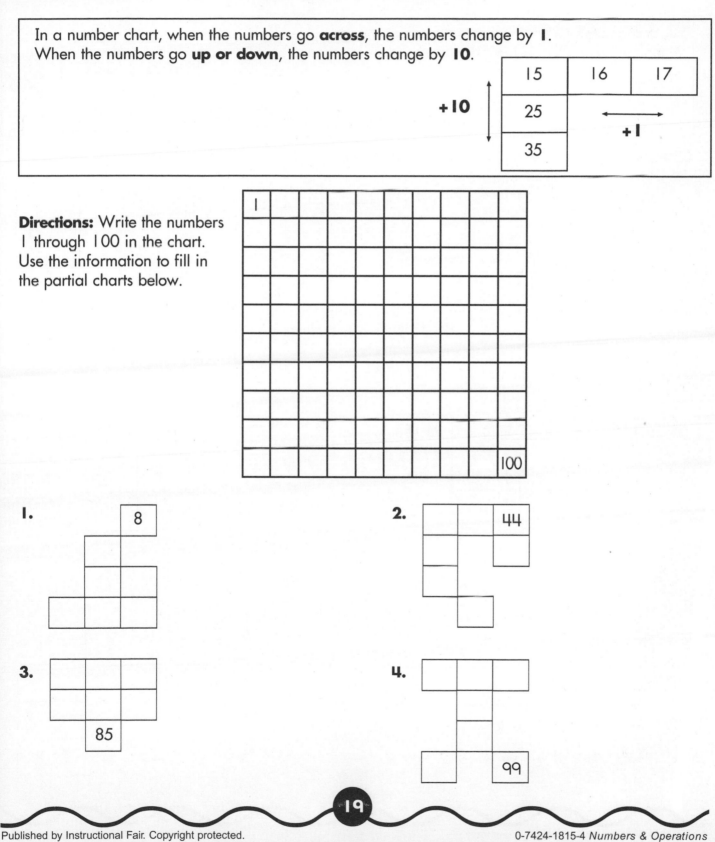

1.

	8

2.

| | 44 |

3.

| 85 |

4.

| 99 |

0-7424-1815-4 *Numbers & Operations*

Name _____ Date _____

Moving Around the Number Charts

When the numbers go **across**, the numbers change by **1**.
When the numbers go **up or down**, the numbers change by **10**.

	+1 →
3,021	3,022
	3,032

+10

Directions: Fill in the partial number charts below.
Use each chart to solve the problem given.

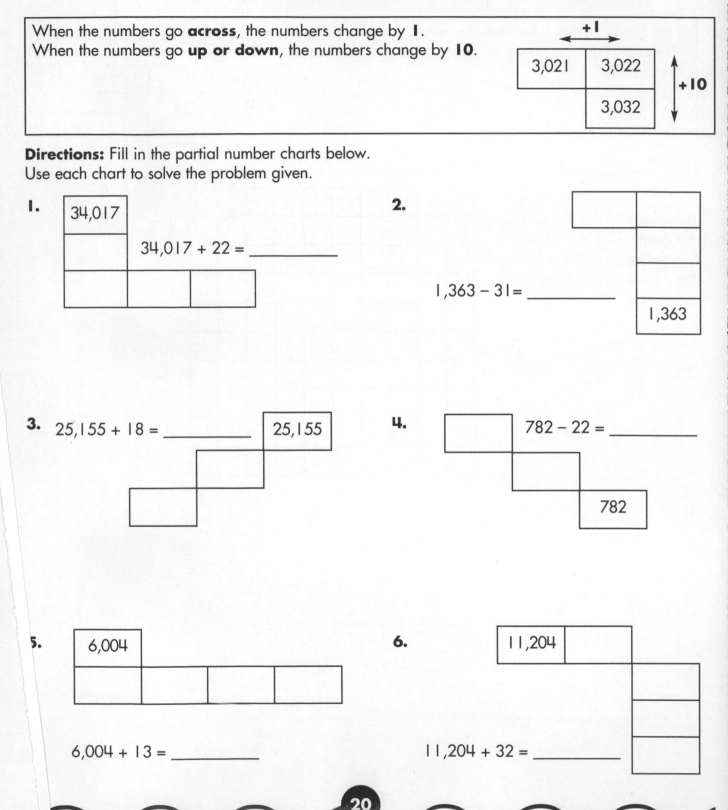

1. 34,017

    34,017 + 22 = _____

2. 1,363 – 31 = _____

    1,363

3. 25,155 + 18 = _____   25,155

4. 782 – 22 = _____

    782

5. 6,004

    6,004 + 13 = _____

6. 11,204

    11,204 + 32 = _____

0-7424-1815-4 *Numbers & Operations*

Name _____ Date _____

Absolute Value of Integers

Integers are counting numbers, their opposites, and zero. Pairs of integers that are the same distance from 0 are called opposites. The absolute value of an integer is its distance from zero on the number line.

Directions: Use the number line to help you solve the problems.

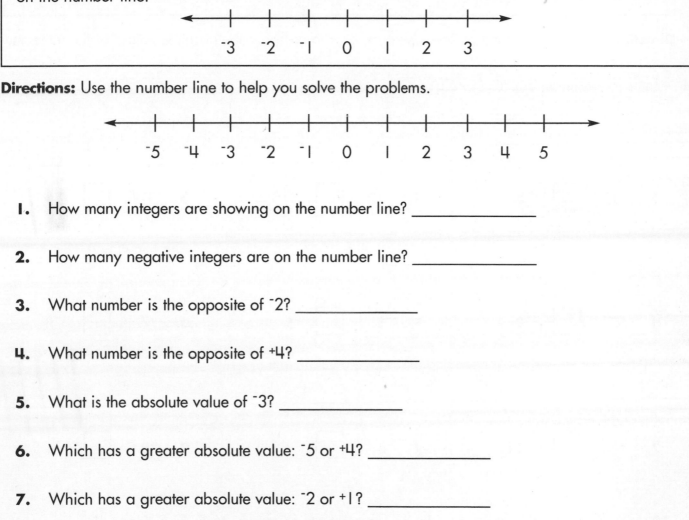

1. How many integers are showing on the number line? _____

2. How many negative integers are on the number line? _____

3. What number is the opposite of ‾2? _____

4. What number is the opposite of ⁺4? _____

5. What is the absolute value of ‾3? _____

6. Which has a greater absolute value: ‾5 or ⁺4? _____

7. Which has a greater absolute value: ‾2 or ⁺1? _____

8. Do you think 0 is positive, negative, or neither? _____

Do More: A frog is at the bottom of a well that is 20 feet deep. If every time it climbs 3 feet up, it slides back down 6 inches, how many times will the frog begin the climb before it is out of the well? Draw a picture of the puzzle. Discuss the puzzle and your illustration with a friend. Explain how you came up with your answer. Did you both come to the same conclusion?

21

Name _____ Date _____

Comparing Integers

Negative integers are less than 0. Positive integers are greater than 0. Zero is neither positive nor negative. Just as with positive numbers, negative numbers increase in absolute value when moving from left to right.

Directions: Look at the number line. Use <, >, or = to compare the absolute values of the integers.

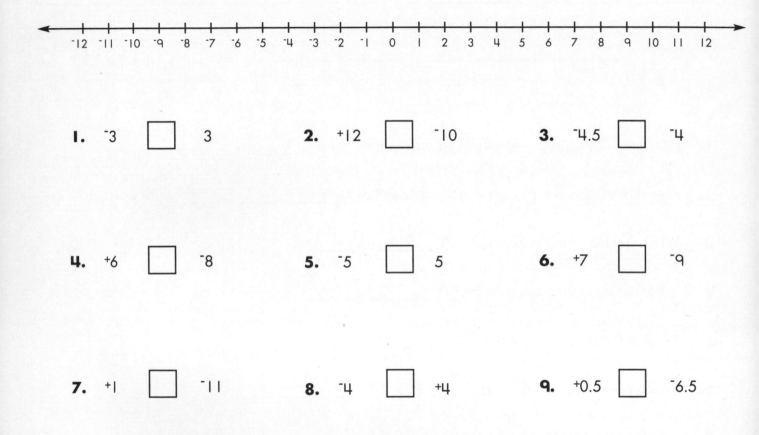

⁻12 ⁻11 ⁻10 ⁻9 ⁻8 ⁻7 ⁻6 ⁻5 ⁻4 ⁻3 ⁻2 ⁻1 0 1 2 3 4 5 6 7 8 9 10 11 12

1. ⁻3 ☐ 3

2. ⁺12 ☐ ⁻10

3. ⁻4.5 ☐ ⁻4

4. ⁺6 ☐ ⁻8

5. ⁻5 ☐ 5

6. ⁺7 ☐ ⁻9

7. ⁺1 ☐ ⁻11

8. ⁻4 ☐ ⁺4

9. ⁺0.5 ☐ ⁻6.5

10. **a.** Place these integers in order on the number line above: ⁺5.5, ⁻0.5, ⁺1$\frac{1}{2}$, ⁻4$\frac{1}{2}$

b. Draw a number line. Place these integers on the number line: ⁻4, ⁺5, ⁺3.5, ⁻6, 0, ⁺4

Do More: The sum of the absolute value of 2 integers is 100. The positive integer has an absolute value 3 times greater than the negative integer. What are the 2 integers? After you have solved the puzzle, discuss your answer with a friend. Did you both come to the same conclusion?

22

Name _____ Date _____

Ordering Integers

```
<----+---+---+---+---+---+---+---+---+---+---+---+---+---+---+---+---->
    -8  -7  -6  -5  -4  -3  -2  -1   0   1   2   3   4   5   6   7   8
```

Directions: Use the number line to help you solve the problems.

1. **a.** Write these numbers in order from least to greatest: $+2.5$, -2.5, $+3.5$, $+3$, 0, -6.5

_____

b. Now place the numbers on a number line.

```
<----+---+---+---+---+---+---+---+---+---+---+---+---+---+---+---+---->
```

2. **a.** Considering the absolute value of each integer, write the following in order from least to greatest: $+1$, -6, -4.5, $+4$, $+5.5$, $+7$

_____

b. Now place the numbers on a number line two different ways—according to absolute value and then as written.

```
<----+---+---+---+---+---+---+---+---+---+---+---+---+---+---+---+---->
```

3. Use <, >, or = to compare the integers.

a. -3 ☐ $+5$ **b.** -6 ☐ $+8$ **c.** $+4$ ☐ -2

d. -3.5 ☐ $+3.5$ **e.** -5 ☐ -2 **f.** $+1.5$ ☐ $+1$

4. Use <, >, or = to compare the absolute values of the integers.

a. -3 ☐ $+5$ **b.** -6 ☐ $+8$ **c.** $+4$ ☐ -2

d. -3.5 ☐ $+3.5$ **e.** -5 ☐ -2 **f.** $+1.5$ ☐ $+1$

Do More: The absolute values of opposite integers have a product of -36. What are the two integers? Draw a number line to prove your answer.

0-7424-1815-4 *Numbers & Operations*

Name _____ Date _____

Decimals

Decimals indicate fractional parts of the whole.
  Tenth means 1 of 10 equal parts of a whole: $\frac{1}{10}$, 10%, or 0.1.
  Thousandth means 1 of 1,000 equal parts of a whole: $\frac{1}{1,000}$, 0.1%, or 0.001.

Directions: Look at the grid. The entire grid represents 1 whole. One row equals $\frac{1}{10}$ of the whole. Written in decimal form, one row is 0.1. One square is $\frac{1}{100}$. Written in decimal form, one square is 0.01. Color the grid by following the step-by-step directions.

1. Color the top and bottom rows red. In decimal form, how much of the grid is red?
    _____

2. Color rows 2, 3, 8, and 9 blue. In decimal form, how much of the grid is blue?
    _____

3. In the center, color a 4-by-4 square green. In decimal form, what part of the grid is green?
    _____

4. Color the rest of the grid purple. In decimal form, how much of the grid is purple?
    _____

Do More: If one of the squares on the grid was divided equally into 10 parts, how would that be written in decimal form?

Published by Instructional Fair. Copyright protected.   0-7424-1815-4 *Numbers & Operations*

Name _____ Date _____

Making Cents of It

Decimals are used to separate dollars and cents. If the grid equals one dollar ($1.00), each row equals one dime ($0.10), and each box equals one penny ($0.01).

Directions: Color the grid by following the step-by-step directions.

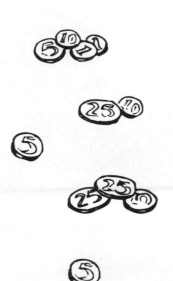

1. Use a red crayon to color squares that represent 5¢.

2. Use a blue crayon to color squares that represent 10¢.

3. Use a yellow crayon to color squares that represent 20¢.

4. Use a purple crayon to color squares that represent 13¢.

5. Use an orange crayon to color squares that represent 33¢.

6. How much money do the uncolored squares represent in total? _____

Do More: If one of the squares on the grid were divided equally into 10 parts, how would you write that as a fraction?

25

Name _____ Date _____

How Much Money?

Directions: Write the value of the dollars and coins. Then answer the questions.

1.

$2.45

2 dollar bills, 1 quarter, 1 nickel, 4 pennies = _____

Enough money to buy this item? _____

If yes, what change will be given? If no, how much more is needed? _____

2.

$6.72

1 5-dollar bill, 6 quarters, 2 dimes, 2 nickels = _____

Enough money to buy this item? _____

If yes, what change will be given? If no, how much more is needed? _____

3.

$5.60

4 dollar bills, 2 half-dollars, 1 dime, 3 pennies = _____

Enough money to buy this item? _____

If yes, what change will be given? If no, how much more is needed? _____

4.

$1.65

4 quarters, 3 dimes, 8 nickels = _____

Enough money to buy this item? _____

If yes, what change will be given? If no, how much more is needed? _____

5.

$5.95

4 dollar bills, 5 quarters, 6 dimes, 1 nickel = _____

Enough money to buy this item? _____

If yes, what change will be given? If no, how much more is needed? _____

0-7424-1815-4 *Numbers & Operations*

Name _____ Date _____

Change, Please

Directions: Find the total value of the coins given. Use a sketch if you need one.

1. 8 quarters

4 dimes

3 nickels

6 pennies

Total value: _____

2. 1 half-dollar

5 quarters

8 nickels

3 pennies

Total value: _____

3. 2 quarters

8 dimes

3 nickels

9 pennies

Total value: _____

4. 3 half-dollars

1 quarter

7 dimes

2 nickels

Total value: _____

5. 1 half-dollar

10 dimes

6 nickels

3 pennies

Total value: _____

6. 7 quarters

5 dimes

1 nickel

9 pennies

Total value: _____

7. 8 quarters

9 dimes

4 nickels

5 pennies

Total value: _____

8. 4 half-dollars

3 quarters

7 nickels

10 pennies

Total value: _____

27

0-7424-1815-4 *Numbers & Operations*

Name _____ Date _____

In the Bank

Directions: Solve the riddles to determine the coins in each bank. There are no bills in the banks, and the coins may be any combination of the following: half-dollar, quarter, dime, nickel, penny. Use a sketch or plastic coins to help you.

1. In my bank, I have 7 coins that total 87¢. Not one of them is a quarter. What coins do I have?

_____

2. My piggy bank has 13 coins that total 94¢. There are 6 nickels. What coins are in my bank?

_____

3. There are 3 types of coins in my bank. I have a total of $1.83 from 12 coins. What are my coins?

_____

4. I have 22 coins in my bank. I feel rich! But after I add them up, they total only 46¢. What are my coins?

_____

5. The coins in my bank total 88¢. There are 2 different types of coins. What is in my bank?

_____

6. I have 5 coins in my bank that total $1.76. There is only 1 quarter in my bank. What are my coins?

_____

7. My bank is filled with coins. I have $2.84 in total and 24 coins. What's in my piggy bank?

_____

8. There are 5 coins in my bank that total $1.02. What are my coins?

_____

Do More: After you have determined the coins for each problem, write an addition sentence to prove you have the correct total.

0-7424-1815-4 *Numbers & Operations*

Name _____ Date _____

Naming the Digits

A decimal is a number with one or more digits to the right of a decimal point.

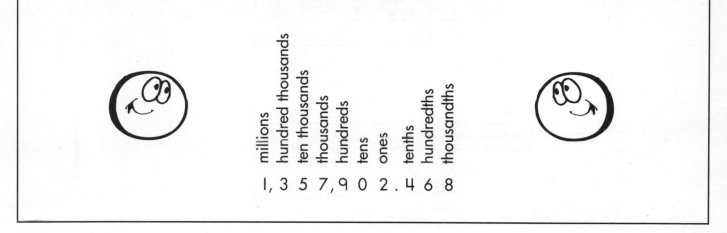

Directions: Use the chart above to help you answer the questions.

1. Which numeral represents the place value of tenths? _____

2. Which numeral represents the place value of thousandths? _____

3. Which numeral represents the place value of hundreds? _____

4. Which numeral represents the place value of hundredths? _____

5. Which numeral represents the place value of thousands? _____

6. Which numeral represents the place value of ten thousands? _____

7. What is the value of the 5?

   _____

8. What is the value of the 1?

   _____

9. What is the value of the 2?

   _____

10. What is the value of the 8?

   _____

Do More: In a number half the size of 1,357,902.468, what place value is represented by 6? Take a guess. Then do the division or use a calculator to find out the answer.

0-7424-1815-4 *Numbers & Operations*

Name _____ Date _____

Density of Population

State	Average number of people per square mile
California	190.8
Texas	64.9
New York	217.9
Florida	239.6
Pennsylvania	265.1

Directions: Statistics are data that is collected, organized, and analyzed. Use the statistics in the table above to solve the word problems.

1. What is the average number of people in 2 square miles in Florida?

_____

2. Which state, when rounded to the nearest hundred, has a density of 300?

_____

3. Which state, when rounded to the nearest ten has a density of 60?

_____

4. Which states, when rounded to the nearest hundreds, have a density of 200?

_____

5. Which 2 states have a total of exactly 330 when added together?

_____

6. Which 3 states have a total density of 772.6?

_____

7. If each number in the table were rounded to the nearest whole number, which 2 states would have an average that ends with a 5?

_____

8. If each number in the table were rounded to the nearest whole number, what state would have an average density that ends in a 0?

_____

30

 0-7424-1815-4 *Numbers & Operations*

Name _____ Date _____

 # Comparing Decimals

Directions: Use <, >, = to compare the decimals.

1.	123.6	☐	124.6	**2.** 52.35	☐	523.5
3.	34.54	☐	34.56	**4.** 10.003	☐	10.030
5.	1,000.5	☐	10,000.4	**6.** 1.89	☐	18.99
7.	0.02	☐	0.002	**8.** 12.11	☐	12.10
9.	0.007	☐	0.07	**10.** 12.22	☐	12.225

Directions: Write the expanded form for the numbers. The first one has been done for you.

11. 65.78 $60 + 5 + 0.7 + 0.08$ _____

12. 94.13 _____

13. 897.431 _____

14. 712.01 _____

15. 11,301.012 _____

16. 8,000.1 _____

17. 50.03 _____

18. 422.02 _____

19. 31,313.013 _____

20. 63,001.12 _____

0-7424-1815-4 *Numbers & Operations*

Name _____ Date _____

Rounding Decimals

Directions: Round to the nearest tenth.

1. 68.13 _____	**2.** 70.39 _____	**3.** 12.07 _____
4. 1.15 _____	**5.** 33.28 _____	**6.** 99.71 _____
7. 885.55 _____	**8.** 988.91 _____	**9.** 601.45 _____

Directions: Round to the nearest hundredth.

10. 1,000.082 _____	**11.** 8.166 _____	**12.** 40.443 _____
13. 9.097 _____	**14.** 220.808 _____	**15.** 0.055 _____
16. 60.811 _____	**17.** 4,531.098 _____	**18.** 66.006 _____

Directions: Round to the nearest thousandth.

19. 0.0097 _____	**20.** 1,111.0109 _____	**21.** 692.8888 _____
22. 7.0121 _____	**23.** 89.0091 _____	**24.** 5,001.0447 _____
25. 8.0066 _____	**26.** 200.7789 _____	**27.** 30.0191 _____

Directions: Choose any three problems on this page and write the answers in word form and expanded form.

28. word form: _____

expanded form: _____

29. word form: _____

expanded form: _____

30. word form: _____

expanded form: _____

0-7424-1815-4 *Numbers & Operations*

Name _____ Date _____

Fractions Are Percents, Too!

A **percentage** is a special ratio that compares a number with one hundred.
Example: 1% means one out of a hundred, so does 0.01, and so does $\frac{1}{100}$.

Directions: Color each circle as indicated by the fraction, decimal, or percent.

1. Color 25% red. What fraction is represented by the colored portion? _____ What decimal is represented by the colored portion?

_____

2. Color $\frac{1}{2}$ green. What decimal is represented by the colored portion? _____ What percent is represented by the colored portion?

_____

3. Color 20% blue. What fraction is represented by the colored portion? _____ What decimal is represented by the colored portion?

_____

4. Color 0.4 red. What fraction is represented by the colored portion? _____ What percentage is represented by the colored portion?

_____

5. Color 50% green. What fraction is represented by the colored portion? _____ What decimal is represented by the colored portion?

_____

6. Color $\frac{2}{5}$ blue. What decimal is represented by the colored portion? _____ What percent is represented by the colored portion?

_____

Do More: Survey 10 people to find out their favorite ice cream flavor. Use the information to create a circle graph. Make a list of the flavors and include the percent represented by each on your graph.

0-7424-1815-4 *Numbers & Operations*

Name _____ Date _____

A Quilt of Percents

Directions: There are 100 squares in the quilt below. Create a patterned quilt by coloring it with the correct percentages: 24% yellow, 16% red, 24% green, 8% blue, 8% orange, 8% pink, 8% black, and 4% purple.

Name _____ Date _____

Household Appliances

Appliance	Percentage of Households in the U.S. That Own
Television	98%
Refrigerator	85%
Oven	90%
Microwave	85%
Dishwasher	45%
Washer	75%
Dryer	60%

Directions: Remember, percent means how many in every 100. If 98% of households own a television, it means that 98 households out of 100 households have one. Use the graph to record the percentage of households that own each kind of appliance.

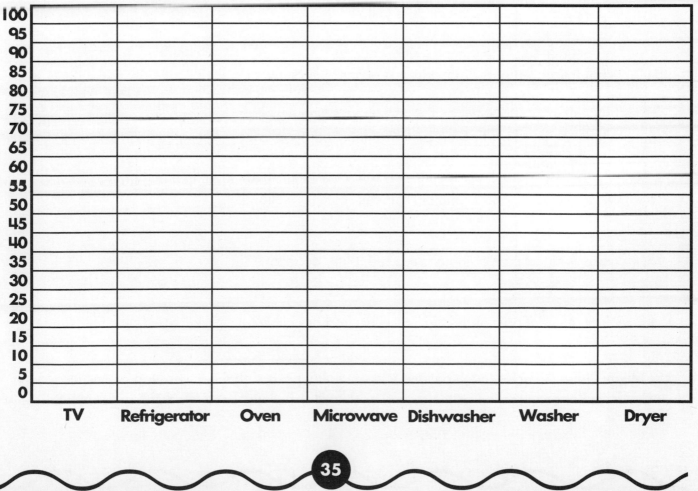

0-7424-1815-4 *Numbers & Operations*

Name _____   Date _____

Decimals Are Fractions

Directions: Each section of the circle represents one tenth, $\frac{1}{10}$, and 0.1. Color 1 section red. Color 2 sections blue. Color 3 sections yellow. Color 4 sections purple.

1. What decimal part of the circle is red? _____

2. What fractional part of the circle is blue? _____

3. What decimal part of the circle is yellow? _____

4. What fractional part of the circle is either blue or red? _____

5. What fractional part of the circle is either red or yellow? _____

6. What fractional part of the circle is red, blue, or yellow? _____

7. What decimal part of the circle is red, blue, or yellow? _____

8. What decimal part of the circle is either red or yellow? _____

Do More: Draw 3 circles, each divided into 10 equal parts. Label each section of one circle with decimals. Label each section of the second circle with fractions. Label the third circle with percents.

0-7424-1815-4 *Numbers & Operations*

Name _____ Date _____

Decimals Are Percentages, Too!

A **percentage** is a special ratio that compares a number with one hundred.
    Example: 1% means one out of a hundred, so does 0.01,
    and so does $\frac{1}{100}$.

Each section of the circle represents 10% of the circle. It can be written in decimals like this: 0.1.

- Color 1 section pink.
- Color 3 sections black
- Color 2 sections orange.
- Color 4 sections brown.

Directions: Use the circle above to answer the questions.

1. What percent of the circle is brown? _____

2. What percent of the circle is black? _____

3. What decimal part of the circle is orange? _____

4. What percent of the circle is either pink or orange? _____

5. What fraction of the circle is either pink or brown? _____

6. What percent of the circle is either black, brown, or pink? _____

Do More: If one section of the circle was equally divided into 10 sections, what percent would each section represent? What fraction? What decimal?

     0-7424-1815-4 *Numbers & Operations*

Name _____ Date _____

Decimals, Fractions, and Percents

Directions: Complete the chart by filling in the missing numbers.

	Decimal	Fraction	Percent
1.	0.2		
2.			40%
3.		$\frac{5}{10}$	
4.	0.05		
5.			70%
6.		$\frac{9}{100}$	
7.	0.33		
8.			1%

Directions: Shade or color each circle to show the decimal, fraction, or percent.

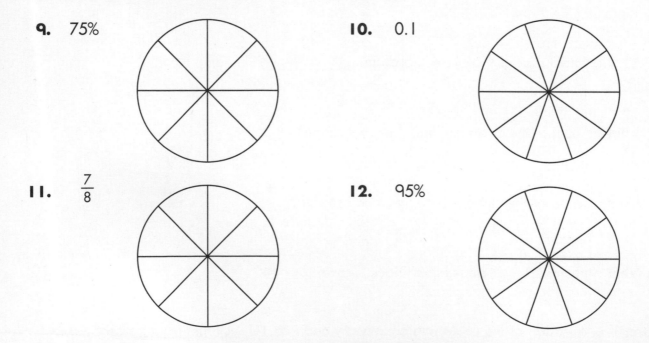

9. 75%

10. 0.1

11. $\frac{7}{8}$

12. 95%

Do More: Write a fraction number sentence for the sum of all the colored sections of the circles above.

0-7424-1815-4 *Numbers & Operations*

Name _____ Date _____

Fraction of an Area

Directions: Look at the diagram. Each section represents a fractional part of the whole. Use the diagram to answer the questions.

1. Which two sections are the same size? _____

2. What fraction does A represent? _____

3. What fraction does B represent? _____

4. Which section is 25% the size of C? _____

5. What is the sum of the fractions represented by B and C? _____

6. What is the difference between the fractions represented by A and D? _____

Do More: What mixed numbers are represented by 6 x B? 7 x C? 20 x A?

0-7424-1815-4 *Numbers & Operations*

Name _____ Date _____

Favorite Pie

Directions: Interview 20 people and find out which pie they like best (apple, cherry, berry, Boston cream, lemon meringue, or pumpkin). Tally each response. Then use the results to color the graph according to the key. Use the graph to compete the word problems on page 41.

Key

green = apple	brown = Boston cream
red = cherry	yellow = lemon meringue
blue = berry	orange = pumpkin

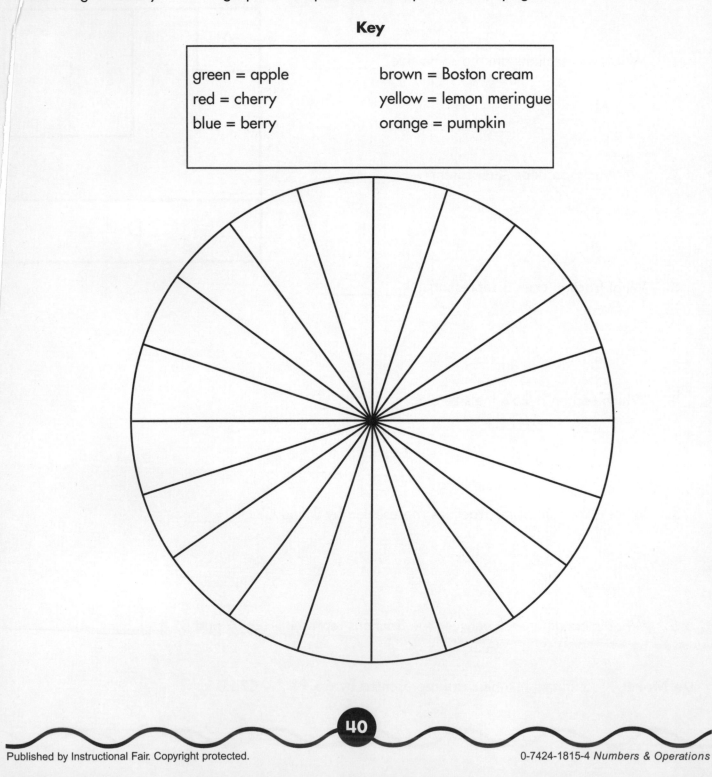

0-7424-1815-4 *Numbers & Operations*

Name _____ Date _____

Favorite Pie

> **Percent** equals 1 out of 100.
> **Fraction** equals the portion compared to the whole.
> **Decimal** represents $\frac{1}{10}$, $\frac{1}{100}$, or $\frac{1}{1,000}$ of the whole.

Directions: Use the circle graph on page 40 to answer the questions.

1. What fraction represents an apple pie preference? _____

2. Write the decimal that represents a cherry pie preference. _____

3. Write the percent that represents a pumpkin pie preference. _____

4. What fraction represents a cherry pie preference? _____

5. Write the percent that represents a cherry pie preference. _____

6. Write the decimal that represents a Boston cream pie preference. _____

7. Write the percent that represents a Boston cream pie preference. _____

8. What fraction represents a Boston cream pie preference? _____

9. Write the percent that represents a berry pie preference. _____

10. Write the decimal that represents a berry pie preference. _____

Do More: Survey 20 more people to find out what color their eyes are. On a separate sheet of paper, tally the eye colors (blue, green, brown, hazel, black). Use the data to create an eye color bar graph.

0-7424-1815-4 *Numbers & Operations*

Like Fractions

The **numerator** is the number above the fraction bar in a fraction.

The **denominator** is the number below the fraction bar in a fraction.

Example: $\dfrac{1}{2}$ ← numerator
← denominator

Directions: When adding fractions with like denominators, find the total of the numerators. To complete this page, begin by coloring the wheel like this: 1 section blue, 2 sections red, 3 sections purple, and 4 sections yellow. Write an addition problem for each color pair. The first one has been done for you.

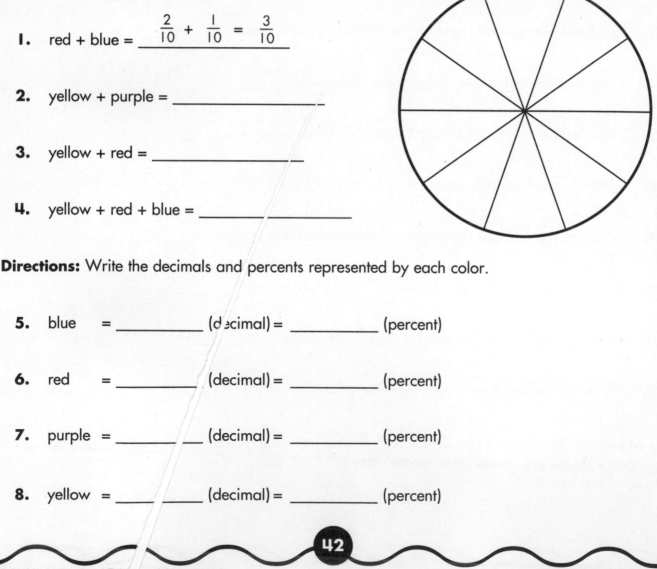

1. red + blue = $\dfrac{2}{10} + \dfrac{1}{10} = \dfrac{3}{10}$

2. yellow + purple = _____

3. yellow + red = _____

4. yellow + red + blue = _____

Directions: Write the decimals and percents represented by each color.

5. blue = _____ (decimal) = _____ (percent)

6. red = _____ (decimal) = _____ (percent)

7. purple = _____ (decimal) = _____ (percent)

8. yellow = _____ (decimal) = _____ (percent)

Published by Instructional Fair. Copyright protected.

Comparing Unlike Fractions

> **Unlike fractions** are fractions that have different denominators.
> Example: $\frac{1}{3}$ and $\frac{1}{4}$

Directions: Follow the coloring directions. Then use the drawings to help you answer the questions.

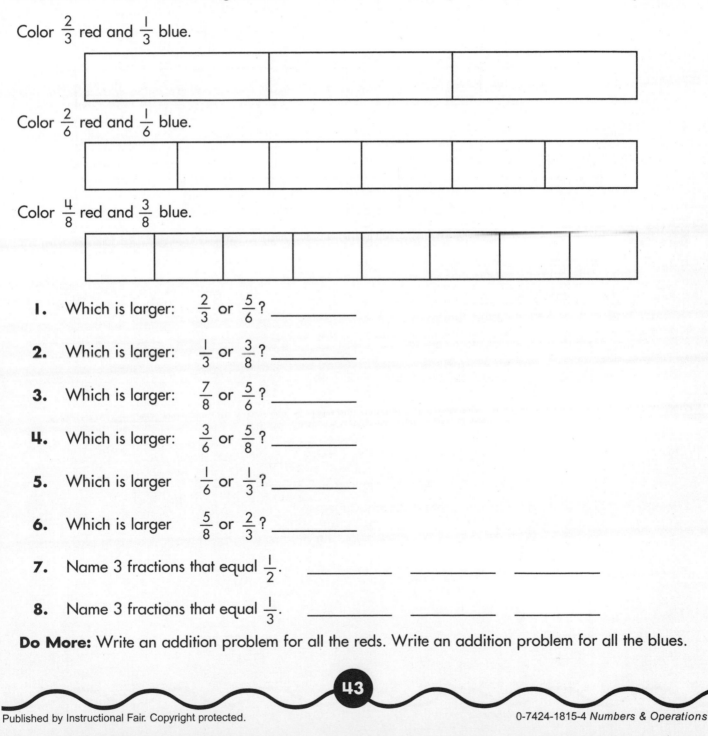

Color $\frac{2}{3}$ red and $\frac{1}{3}$ blue.

Color $\frac{2}{6}$ red and $\frac{1}{6}$ blue.

Color $\frac{4}{8}$ red and $\frac{3}{8}$ blue.

1. Which is larger: $\frac{2}{3}$ or $\frac{5}{6}$? _____

2. Which is larger: $\frac{1}{3}$ or $\frac{3}{8}$? _____

3. Which is larger: $\frac{7}{8}$ or $\frac{5}{6}$? _____

4. Which is larger: $\frac{3}{6}$ or $\frac{5}{8}$? _____

5. Which is larger $\frac{1}{6}$ or $\frac{1}{3}$? _____

6. Which is larger $\frac{5}{8}$ or $\frac{2}{3}$? _____

7. Name 3 fractions that equal $\frac{1}{2}$. _____ _____ _____

8. Name 3 fractions that equal $\frac{1}{3}$. _____ _____ _____

Do More: Write an addition problem for all the reds. Write an addition problem for all the blues.

0-7424-1815-4 *Numbers & Operations*

Name _____ Date _____

Equivalent Fractions

> **Equivalent fractions** are fractions with the same value.
> They name the same number.
>   Example: $\frac{1}{2} = \frac{2}{4}$

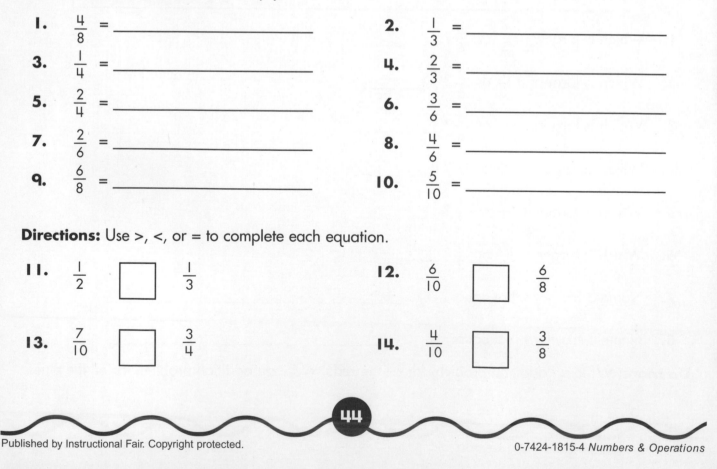

Directions: How many equivalent fractions can you list? Write as many as you can for each fraction. Use the chart above to help you.

1. $\frac{4}{8}$ = _____

2. $\frac{1}{3}$ = _____

3. $\frac{1}{4}$ = _____

4. $\frac{2}{3}$ = _____

5. $\frac{2}{4}$ = _____

6. $\frac{3}{6}$ = _____

7. $\frac{2}{6}$ = _____

8. $\frac{4}{6}$ = _____

9. $\frac{6}{8}$ = _____

10. $\frac{5}{10}$ = _____

Directions: Use >, <, or = to complete each equation.

11. $\frac{1}{2}$ ☐ $\frac{1}{3}$

12. $\frac{6}{10}$ ☐ $\frac{6}{8}$

13. $\frac{7}{10}$ ☐ $\frac{3}{4}$

14. $\frac{4}{10}$ ☐ $\frac{3}{8}$

0-7424-1815-4 *Numbers & Operations*

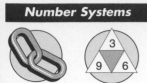

Name _____ Date _____

Unlike Fractions

The **least common denominator** is used when renaming fractions so that they have the same denominator. The numbers that are multiples of both denominators are the common denominators. The smallest of the common denominators is the least common denominator.

Example: **1.** For $\frac{1}{8}$ and $\frac{7}{10}$, 40 is the least common denominator.

2. Once you know the least common denominator, multiply each fraction by a form of 1 to make each denominator equal 40. In this example, $\frac{5}{5}$ and $\frac{4}{4}$ are both forms of 1 (a fraction with the same numerator and denominator).

$$\frac{1}{8} \times \frac{5}{5} = \frac{5}{40}$$

$$\frac{7}{10} \times \frac{4}{4} = \frac{28}{40}$$

3. Once fractions have a common denominator, you can easily compare them.

Directions: Color the first wheel like this: 1 section red, 2 sections blue, 3 sections orange, and 2 sections black. Color the second wheel like this: 1 section pink, 3 sections orange, 4 sections blue, 2 sections red. Look at each color and estimate its fractional part. Then write the fractions for each color and find the sums. Use the least common denominator to reduce the fractions to the smallest terms.

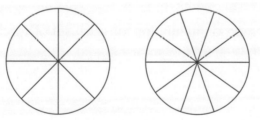

1. all the red = $\dfrac{1}{8} + \dfrac{2}{10} = \dfrac{5}{40} + \dfrac{8}{40} = \dfrac{13}{40}$ _____

2. all the blue = _____

3. all the orange = _____

4. all the black + all the pink = _____

5. all the red + all the blue = _____

6. all the orange + all the black = _____

0-7424-1815-4 *Numbers & Operations*

Name _____ Date _____

Least Common Denominator

> Remember, the **least common denominator** is the least common multiple of the denominators of two or more fractions.
>
> Example: For $\frac{1}{3}$ and $\frac{1}{4}$, 12 is the least common denominator.
>
> $$\frac{1}{3} \times \frac{4}{4} = \frac{4}{12}$$
>
> $$\frac{1}{4} \times \frac{3}{3} = \frac{3}{12}$$

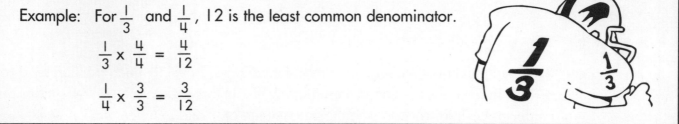

Directions: Find the least common multiple for each of the number pairs. The first one has been done for you.

1. 3, 5 = __15__   **2.** 4, 6 = _____   **3.** 2, 7 = _____

4. 2, 9 = _____   **5.** 3, 4 = _____   **6.** 3, 10 = _____

7. 2, 5 = _____   **8.** 3, 8 = _____   **9.** 5, 6 = _____

Directions: Find the least common denominator for each set of fractions. Rewrite the problem and find the sum or difference.

10. $\frac{1}{2} + \frac{1}{3} =$

11. $\frac{1}{4} - \frac{1}{8} =$

12. $\frac{4}{5} - \frac{1}{10} =$

13. $\frac{1}{12} + \frac{5}{6} =$

Do More: On Monday you buy a whole pie and eat half. Every day that week, you eat half of what is left until Sunday, when you finish off the pie. What fraction of the pie will you eat on Sunday? Prove your answer with drawings for each day of the week.

0-7424-1815-4 *Numbers & Operations*

Name _____ Date _____

Mixed Numbers

A **mixed number** is a whole number and a fraction. An **improper fraction** is a fraction with a numerator greater than or equal to the denominator.

To change a mixed number to an improper fraction:

1. Change the whole number to a fraction.
2. Add the fractions.

   Example: $3\frac{7}{8}$ is a mixed number.

   $$3 = \frac{24}{8}$$
   $$\frac{24}{8} + \frac{7}{8} = \frac{31}{8}$$

To change an improper fraction to a mixed number:

1. Divide the numerator by the denominator.
2. Write the quotient as the whole number part. Write the remainder over the divisor.

   Example: $\frac{31}{8}$ is an improper fraction.

   $$31 \div 8 = 3 \text{ R}7$$
   $$3\frac{7}{8}$$

Directions: Change the mixed numbers to improper fractions.

1. $3\frac{1}{4}$ = _____

2. $1\frac{1}{3}$ = _____

3. $4\frac{1}{2}$ = _____

4. $2\frac{5}{8}$ = _____

5. $2\frac{1}{5}$ = _____

6. $4\frac{2}{3}$ = _____

Directions: Change the improper fractions to mixed numbers.

7. $\frac{10}{3}$ = _____

8. $\frac{21}{4}$ = _____

9. $\frac{13}{2}$ = _____

10. $\frac{18}{5}$ = _____

11. $\frac{15}{7}$ = _____

12. $\frac{9}{4}$ = _____

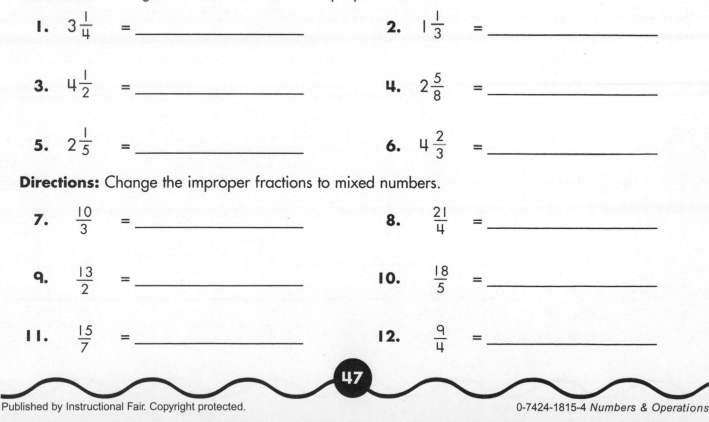

47

Name _____ Date _____

Number Line Fractions, Decimals, and Percents

Directions: Order the fractions, decimals, and percents given from smallest to greatest. Then place them in the correct order on the number line.

1. $\frac{6}{8}$, 0.15, 25%, $\frac{1}{3}$ _____

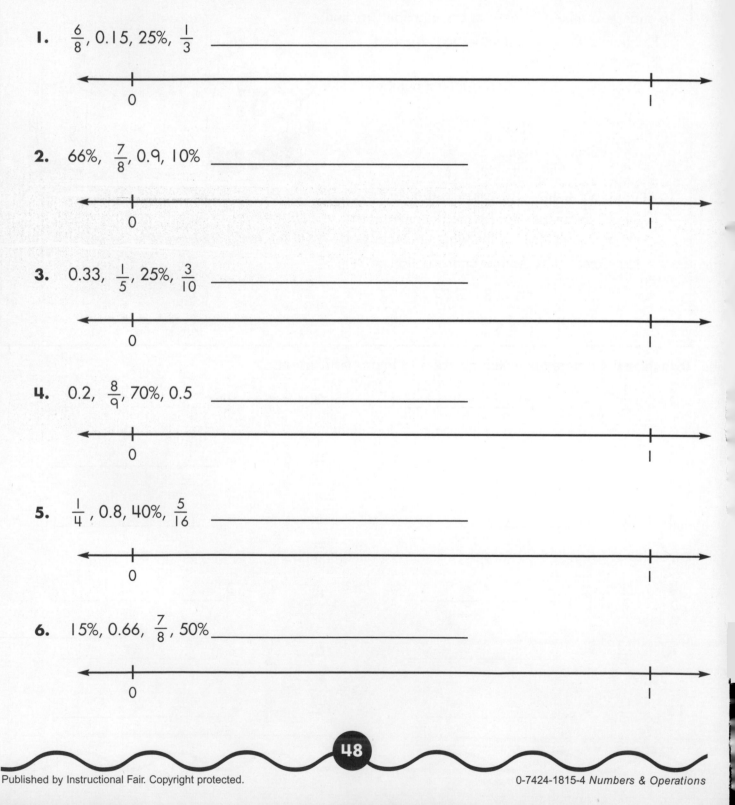

2. 66%, $\frac{7}{8}$, 0.9, 10% _____

3. 0.33, $\frac{1}{5}$, 25%, $\frac{3}{10}$ _____

4. 0.2, $\frac{8}{9}$, 70%, 0.5 _____

5. $\frac{1}{4}$, 0.8, 40%, $\frac{5}{16}$ _____

6. 15%, 0.66, $\frac{7}{8}$, 50% _____

0-7424-1815-4 *Numbers & Operations*

Name _____ Date _____

Least Common Multiple

Directions: Find the product of each pair of numbers. Then find all the multiples of each number up to their product. Circle the least common multiple of the pair. The first one has been done for you.

1. 6, 10

   6 x 10 = 60

   6: 6, 12, 18, 24, 30, 36, 42, 48, 54, 60

   10: 10, 20, 30, 40, 50, 60

2. 4, 5

3. 3, 5

4. 5, 6

5. 6, 8

6. 3, 7

7. 4, 14

8. 3, 15

9. 5, 9

10. 6, 9

Do More: Solve this problem: Paulo, Leo, and Miko are buddies at summer camp. It takes Paulo 6 minutes to walk around the lake. It takes Leo 9 minutes to walk around the lake. It takes Miko 12 minutes to complete the trip around the lake. All 3 boys begin walking at the same time and keep walking until they are all back at the starting point. How long will it be before they are all together again at the starting point? To prove your answer, illustrate the puzzle.

0-7424-1815-4 *Numbers & Operations*

Name _____ Date _____

Finding Factors

> A **factor** of a number is any value that goes into the number evenly (no remainders).
>
> A **composite** number has factors other than 1 and itself.

Directions: There are several "tricks" for finding factors of large numbers. You may be familiar with some of them already. Answer the questions below, using a 100 chart (see page 19) for reference.

1. Complete the following statements.

    a. A composite number will have 2 for a factor if _____.

    b. A composite number will have 5 for a factor if _____.

    c. A composite number will have 10 for a factor if _____.

2. Circle all the multiples of 3 on the 100 chart. Find the sum of the digits in each multiple of 9. What do you notice? _____

3. Put a square around all the multiples of 9 on the 100 chart. Find the sum of the digits in each multiple of 9. What do you notice? _____

4. A composite number will have 4 for a factor if 4 is a factor of the last 2 digits of the number.

    a. Which of the following numbers are divisible by 4? Use the trick to answer the question.
        1282,464 272   346   388   2,300   718   4,512

    b. Test the trick. Divide each of the numbers in part a. by 4. Does the trick work for each number?

Do More: Use the 100 chart to examine multiples of 6, 7, and 8. Can you find any patterns? Do you think there is a trick for each number?

     0-7424-1815-4 *Numbers & Operations*

Name _____ Date _____

Positively Prime

> A **prime** number's only factors are 1 and itself.
> Example: 3 is a prime number.
> 3 x 1 = 3

Directions: Answer the questions.

1. Can an even number be prime? Explain.

_____

2. Are all odd numbers prime? Explain.

_____

3. Is the product of 2 prime numbers also prime? Explain.

_____

4. Look at a multiplication table (see page69). What can you say about every number inside the table?

_____

5. Consider the number 91.
   a. Is 2 a factor? _____
   b. Is 3, 6, or 9 a factor? _____
   c. Is 4 or 8 a factor? _____
   d. Is 5 or 10 a factor? _____
   e. Do you think 91 is prime? _____
   f. Try dividing 91 by prime numbers larger than 10. Can you find a factor? _____
   g. Is 91 prime? _____

6. Find all the prime numbers between 1 and 100.

Do More: Explain your strategy for deciding whether or not a number is prime.
Do you use any "tricks" to save time?

0-7424-1815-4 *Numbers & Operations*

Name _____ Date _____

Greatest Common Factor

Factors are the numbers that can be evenly divided into a number.

To find the **greatest common factor** of 12 and 30, list all the numbers that can be divided into each number. The largest will be the greatest common factor.

Example:
10 = 1, 2, 5, (10)
30 = 1, 2, 3, 5, 6, (10) 15

Directions: Study the example for finding the greatest common factor of 10 and 30. Then find the greatest common factor of each number pair below. The first one has been started for you.

1. 30, 50
30: 1, 2, 3, 5, 6, 10, 15, 30
50: 1, 2, 5, 10, 25, 50
greatest common factor _____

2. 18, 42
18 _____
42 _____
greatest common factor _____

3. 10, 15
10 _____
15 _____
greatest common factor _____

4. 8, 40
8 _____
40 _____
greatest common factor _____

5. 12, 20
12 _____
20 _____
greatest common factor _____

6. 16, 64
16 _____
64 _____
greatest common factor _____

0-7424-1815-4 *Numbers & Operations*

Check Your Skills—Number Systems

1. What is the absolute value of ⁻4? _____

2. What is the absolute value of ⁺6? _____

3. Write ten million eight hundred thousand fifty-six using numerals. _____

4. Round 3,568,986 to the nearest hundred thousand. _____

5. **a.** Write 8,976,424 in expanded form.
   _____

   b. What is the value of the 7? _____

6. In 156.897, which numeral represents hundredths? _____

7. How many of the squares equals 0.1? _____

8. Complete the chart.

Decimal	Fraction	Percent
0.5		
	$\frac{1}{100}$	

9. Write three fractions that are equivalent to $\frac{1}{2}$. _____

10. Which is larger: $\frac{3}{6}$ or $\frac{5}{8}$? _____

11. What is the least common denominator of $\frac{1}{2}$ and $\frac{5}{7}$? _____

12. What is the least common multiple of 6 and 10? _____

13. What is the greatest common factor of 48 and 60? _____

14. **a.** Shade 40%.

    b. What percent of the bar is not shaded? _____

    c. What fraction of the bar is shaded? _____

    d. What decimal represents the shaded portion? _____

Published by Instructional Fair. Copyright protected.   0-7424-1815-4 *Numbers & Operations*

Commutative Property of Addition

The **commutative property** of addition says that changing
the order of the addends does not change the sum.
    Example: $613 + 257 = 870$
                $257 + 613 = 870$

Directions: Find the sums of each set of numbers. For each group, list yet another equation using the same addends.

1. $235 + 5 + 71 + 1 =$ _____
        $71 + 235 + 1 + 5 =$ _____

        _____

2. $314 + 80 + 69 + 81 =$ _____
        $81 + 80 + 69 + 314 =$ _____

        _____

3. $132 + 89 + 73 + 50 =$ _____
        $73 + 132 + 89 + 50 =$ _____

        _____

4. $704 + 68 + 21 + 50 =$ _____
        $21 + 704 + 68 + 50 =$ _____

        _____

5. $78 + 93 + 5 + 7 =$ _____
        $93 + 7 + 5 + 78 =$ _____

        _____

6. $84 + 62 + 311 + 8 =$ _____
        $62 + 8 + 311 + 84 =$ _____

        _____

7. $814 + 79 + 9 + 11 =$ _____
        $814 + 11 + 79 + 9 =$ _____

        _____

8. $533 + 94 + 84 + 7 =$ _____
        $7 + 533 + 84 + 94 =$ _____

        _____

Think: Which problem in each group above was easiest for you to solve? How can understanding the commutative property help you find an easier way to solve problems?

0-7424-1815-4 *Numbers & Operations*

Name _____ Date _____

Associative Property of Addition

The **associative property** of addition says that the way addends
are grouped does not change the sum.

Example: $(901 + 4) + 45 = 950$

$901 + (4 + 45) = 950$

Directions: Find the sums. Begin by adding the numbers in the parentheses. Then add that sum
to the third number.

1. $(20 + 140) + 15 =$ _____

2. $(140 + 15) + 20 =$ _____

3. $(20 + 15) + 140 =$ _____

4. Draw a picture or write an example to prove the associative property of addition.

5. How would you explain the associative property to a friend who was not in class the
day you learned about it?

_____

_____

6. The commutative property of addition states that changing the order of the addends
does not affect their sum $(8 + 5 = 5 + 8)$. Draw a picture or write an example to prove
the commutative property of addition.

7. How would you explain the commutative property to a friend who was not in class the
day you learned about it?

_____

_____

0-7424-1815-4 *Numbers & Operatio*

Name _____ Date _____

It All Adds Up

Directions: Put checks in the chart to make addition equations with the appropriate sums. Use the fewest amount of checks possible. Write each equation. The first two have been done for you.

sum	1	4	16	64	equation
1. 20		✓	✓		$4 + 16 = 20$
2. 70	✓ ✓	✓		✓	$(1 + 1) + 4 + 64 = 70$
3. 33					
4. 40					
5. 99					
6. 130					
7. 88					
8. 18					
9. 36					
10. 207					
11. 400					
12. 876					

Do More: Using as few numbers as possible, write a combination of the numbers 1, 4, 16, and 64 with a sum of 1,000.

0-7424-1815-4 *Numbers & Operations*

Name _____ Date _____

Matching Sums and Products

Directions: Find the sums and products. Then draw a line connecting the matching equations.

1. $5 + 5 + 5 + 5 + 5 =$ **a.** $7 \times 4 =$

2. $7 + 7 + 7 + 7 =$ **b.** $6 \times 7 =$

3. $8 + 8 + 8 + 8 + 8 =$ **c.** $9 \times 5 =$

4. $6 + 6 + 6 + 6 + 6 + 6 + 6 =$ **d.** $8 \times 7 =$

5. $9 + 9 + 9 + 9 + 9 =$ **e.** $5 \times 5 =$

6. $8 + 8 + 8 + 8 + 8 + 8 + 8 =$ **f.** $8 \times 5 =$

7. $6 + 6 + 6 + 6 + 6 + 6 + 6 + 6 =$ **g.** $7 \times 5 =$

8. $7 + 7 + 7 + 7 + 7 =$ **h.** $5 \times 4 =$

9. $5 + 5 + 5 + 5 =$ **i.** $4 \times 8 =$

10. $4 + 4 + 4 + 4 + 4 + 4 + 4 + 4 =$ **j.** $6 \times 8 =$

11. $6 + 6 + 6 + 6 + 6 =$ **k.** $7 \times 9 =$

12. $9 + 9 + 9 + 9 + 9 + 9 + 9 + 9 =$ **l.** $4 \times 9 =$

13. $4 + 4 + 4 + 4 + 4 + 4 =$ **m.** $4 \times 6 =$

14. $7 + 7 + 7 + 7 + 7 + 7 + 7 + 7 + 7 =$ **n.** $9 \times 8 =$

15. $4 + 4 + 4 + 4 + 4 + 4 + 4 + 4 + 4 =$ **o.** $6 \times 5 =$

Do More: What is $3 \times 3 \times 3$?

     0-7424-1815-4 *Numbers & Operations*

Name _____ Date _____

Distance, Rate, and Time

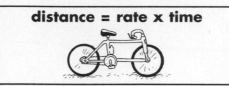

distance = rate x time

Directions: Answer the following questions using the formula for distance given above.

1. Brianna rode her bike at an average speed of 10.8 mph. It took her 2.5 hours to ride to her grandmother's house.

   a. How far away does her grandmother live? Show your work. _____

   b. What math operation did you use to find the answer? Why? _____

2. On the return trip, Brianna averaged only 9 mph. To find the time of her trip, the problem needs to be worked backwards.

   a. How long did it take Brianna to get home? Show your work. _____

   b. Does your answer make sense? Why or why not? _____

   c. Write an equation showing how to find the time if the distance and rate are known.

   time = _____

3. The next day Brianna is tired. She rides her bike to the store to get her grandmother some chocolates. The trip is a total of 20 miles and it takes her 2.5 hours.

   a. How fast did Brianna travel? _____

   b. What math operation did you use to find the answer? Why? _____

Think: How is the equation for time related to the equation for distance?

Published by Instructional Fair. Copyright protected.

0-7424-1815-4 *Numbers & Operations*

Name _____ Date _____

Commutative Property of Multiplication

The **commutative property** of multiplication states that changing the order of the factors does not change the product.

Example: 4 x 3 = 12
            3 x 4 = 12

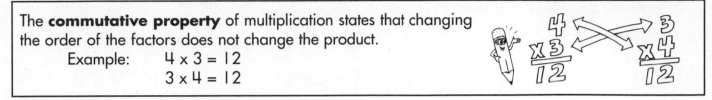

Directions: Use what you know about the commutative property of multiplication to answer the questions below.

1. Write the number sentence that each picture models.

a. 8 x 4 = _____   **b.** _____

2. Julia collects marbles. She has 5 small boxes, each holding 3 marbles.

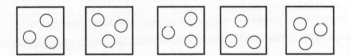

a. How many marbles does Julia have? _____

b. Write a number sentence that models the problem. _____

c. Draw a picture to show how she could arrange the marbles if she had only 3 boxes.

d. Write a number sentence that models the problem. _____

Think: How are the pairs of equations in each problem related?

0-7424-1815-4 *Numbers & Operations*

Name _____ Date _____

Distributive Property

Directions: Explore the distributive property of multiplication over addition by answering the following questions.

1. Write the number sentences that model the picture.

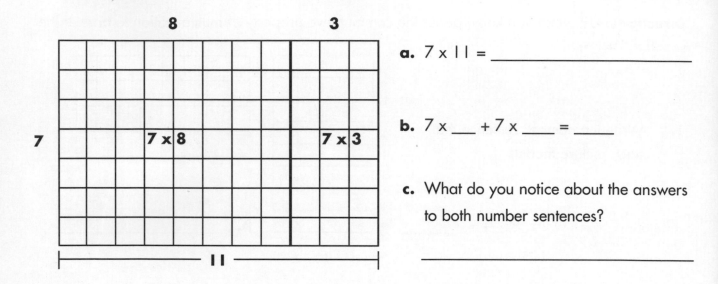

a. $7 \times 11 =$ _____

b. $7 \times$ ___ $+ 7 \times$ ___ $=$ ____

c. What do you notice about the answers to both number sentences?

_____

2. On the back of this paper, draw a picture that shows $5 \times 13 =$ _____.

a. Show how you can divide the rectangle you drew above into 2 smaller rectangles. Write the number sentence that models the picture.

b. Divide the rectangle differently and write the number sentence.

c. What is true about the answers to each number sentence?

Do More: Write a definition for the distributive property using your own words.

0-7424-1815-4 *Numbers & Operations*

Name _____ Date _____

Multiplication Is the Opposite of Division

Directions: For each grid, list two addition, multiplication, and division equations. Example: Begin the first one with 2 + 2 + 2 = 6.

1.

addition _____ _____

multiplication _____ _____

division _____ _____

2.

addition _____ _____

multiplication _____ _____

division _____ _____

3.

addition _____ _____

multiplication _____ _____

division _____ _____

4.

addition _____ _____

multiplication _____ _____

division _____ _____

5.

addition _____ _____

multiplication _____ _____

division _____ _____

Do More: Draw a picture to prove that $81 \div 9 = 9$.

0-7424-1815-4 *Numbers & Operations*

Name _____ Date _____

Opposites

> The **associative property** of multiplication says that
> the way factors are grouped does not change the product.
>
> Example: $(4 \times 5) \times 2 = 40$
>
> $4 \times (5 \times 2) = 40$

Directions: Find the products.

1. $(5 \times 8) \times 2 = $ _____

$5 \times (8 \times 2) = $ _____

2. $6 \times (5 \times 1) = $ _____

$(6 \times 5) \times 1 = $ _____

3. $(3 \times 8) \times 2 = $ _____

$3 \times (8 \times 2) = $ _____

4. $6 \times (3 \times 1) = $ _____

$(6 \times 3) \times 1 = $ _____

5. $2 \times (3 \times 2) = $ _____

$(2 \times 3) \times 2 = $ _____

6. $8 \times (4 \times 1) = $ _____

$(8 \times 4) \times 1 = $ _____

Directions: Find the products. Then write a division equation for each one. The first one has been done for you.

7. $6 \times 9 = $ ___54___ $54 \div 9 = 6$

8. $4 \times 10 = $ _____   _____

9. $5 \times 7 = $ _____   _____

10. $8 \times 9 = $ _____   _____

11. $11 \times 9 = $ _____   _____

12. $6 \times 12 = $ _____   _____

13. $5 \times 9 = $ _____   _____

14. $3 \times 9 = $ _____   _____

15. $2 \times 9 = $ _____   _____

16. $4 \times 12 = $ _____   _____

17. $6 \times 7 = $ _____   _____

18. $11 \times 10 = $ _____   _____

19. $4 \times 9 = $ _____   _____

20. $7 \times 9 = $ _____   _____

21. $7 \times 4 = $ _____   _____

22. $2 \times 12 = $ _____   _____

0-7424-1815-4 *Numbers & Operations*

Name _____ Date _____

Complete the Charts

> When you add numbers, the result is the **sum**.
> When you subtract numbers, the result is the **difference**.
> When you multiply numbers, the result is the **product**.
> When you divide numbers, the result is the **quotient**.

Directions: Complete the charts by finding the sum, difference, product, and quotient for each number pair. The first one has been started for you.

1.

	8, 2	10, 5	12, 4	20, 2	50, 10
sum	10				
difference	6				
product					
quotient					

2.

	144, 6	99, 3	450, 18	612, 4	1,053, 13
sum					
difference					
product					
quotient					

Do More: What number pair has the same sum, difference, and quotient? Reproduce the vocabulary cards at the back of this book to practice these and other math terms.

0-7424-1815-4 *Numbers & Operations*

Name _____ Date _____

Exploring Exponents

An **exponent** is a number that tells how many times the base is used as a factor.

a. $3^2 = 3 \times 3 = 9$ **b.** $3^3 = 3 \times 3 \times 3 = 27$ **c.** $3^4 = (3 \times 3 \times 3) \times 3 = 81$

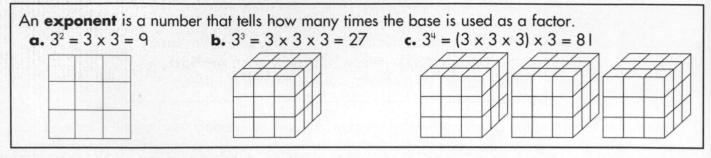

Directions: Use the pictures above to help you solve the word problems below.

1. You have 3 colors of posterboard: red, blue, and yellow. You have 3 packs of each color.
   a. Which picture will help solve the problem? _____
   b. How many sheets of posterboard do you have? _____

2. You have 3 patterns of posterboard: solid, striped, and checked. You have 3 colors of all 3 patterns. There are 3 sheets per packet.
   a. Which picture will help solve the problem? _____
   b. How many sheets of posterboard do you have? _____

3. On Monday, Tuesday, and Wednesday, you worked for 3 hours. You earned $3 an hour and worked these hours for 3 weeks.
   a. Which picture will help solve the problem? _____
   b. What were your total earnings? _____

4. Write a word problem that could be illustrated by picture a. Trade problems with a friend and solve.

   _____

   _____

   _____

Do More: You find a bottle with a genie in it. The genie says you can have 1 wish today, 2 wishes tomorrow, 3 wishes the next day, and so on for the next 7 days. At the end of the week, how many wishes will you have?

Published by Instructional Fair. Copyright protected.   0-7424-1815-4 *Numbers & Operations*

Name _____ Date _____

Down on the Farm

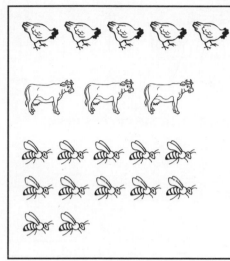

Five hens lay 25 eggs per week.

Three cows give 15 gallons of milk per week.

Twelve bees make 1 tablespoon of honey during their lifetime.

Directions: Use the data above to solve the problems. Show your work.

1. How many gallons of milk does each cow give per week? _____

2. How many eggs will 10 hens lay in 2 weeks? _____

3. How much honey does 1 bee make during its lifetime? _____

4. How long will it take 10 hens to lay 500 eggs? _____

5. How long will it take 1 dozen cows to give 240 gallons of milk? _____

6. There are 16 tablespoons in 1 cup. How many bees will it take to make 1 cup of honey? _____

7. How long will it take 15 hens to lay 150 eggs? _____

8. How much milk will 6 cows give in 3 weeks? _____

Do More: If milk sells for 50¢ a gallon and eggs are 90¢ per dozen, how much per week will the farmer make if he has 200 hens and 120 cows?

0-7424-1815-4 *Numbers & Operations*

Name _____ Date _____

Mable's Outfits

Directions: Mable has 3 blouses, 3 skirts, and 2 dresses in her suitcase. Use the clothes in her suitcase and facts found below to solve each word problem. Show your work.

1. How many different skirt-and-blouse outfits can Mable wear? _____

2. How many different skirt-and-blouse or dress outfits can Mable wear? _____

3. Mable bought a new sweater on her trip. She can add the sweater or not add the sweater to each of her outfits. What is the total number of different ways she can dress now? _____

4. Mable spilled hot chocolate on one of her blouses and cannot wear it. Counting the dresses and new sweater, how many different outfits can she make without one of the blouses? _____

5. Mable bought a new hat. Combining hat or no hat, sweater or no sweater, how many dress outfits can Mable make? _____

6. Mable combines all her clothes (except for the stained blouse), the hat, and the sweater. How many different combinations can be made? _____

Do More: Approximately how many shirts do you have? Approximately how many skirts or pairs of pants do you have? If you don't consider matching colors, how many days could you dress without ever wearing the same outfit?

Published by Instructional Fair. Copyright protected.

0-7424-1815-4 *Numbers & Operations*

Name _____ Date _____

Eric's Sandwich Party

Directions: Eric is having a sandwich party. He bought bread, ham, cheese, salami, lettuce, mustard, and mayonnaise. Use the sandwich fixings to solve the problems. Write an equation for each one or draw pictures to help you.

1. Using all 4 ingredients (ham, cheese, salami, and lettuce) on each sandwich, how many different kinds of sandwiches can be made with none, 1, or both condiments?

    _____

2. Using mustard, mayonaise, mustard and mayonaise, or no condiments, how many different kinds of sandwiches can be made with 1 ingredient (ham, cheese, lettuce, or salami)?

    _____

3. Using mustard, mayonaise, mustard and mayonaise, or no condiments, how many different kinds of sandwiches can be made with only 2 ingredients?

    _____

4. Using mustard, mayonaise, mustard and mayonaise, or no condiments, how many different kinds of sandwiches can be made combining any number of the 4 ingredients?

    _____

5. Eric's best friend Gary loves turkey sandwiches, so Eric goes out and buys some turkey. Using all 5 ingredients (ham, turkey, cheese, salami, and lettuce) on each sandwich, how many different kinds of sandwiches can be made with none, 1, or both condiments?

    _____

6. Using mustard, mayonaise, mustard and mayonaise, or no condiments, how many different kinds of sandwiches can be made with 1 ingredient (ham, turkey, cheese, lettuce, or salami)? _____

Do More: Meet with a friend who has completed this page to compare your answers. Explain to your friend how you arrived at each of your answers.

0-7424-1815-4 *Numbers & Operations*

Name _____ Date _____

Biscuit Pizzas

Ingredients	Directions
2 cans of ready-to-bake biscuits	**I.** Remove biscuits from can and roll into one large ball. Spread out on cookie sheet to make a crust.
I cup shredded cheese	
$\frac{1}{4}$ cup chopped peppers	**2.** Sprinkle cheese, vegetables, and meat over dough.
$\frac{1}{2}$ cup chopped tomatoes	
$\frac{1}{4}$ cup chopped onion	**3.** In a blender, mix eggs, milk, salt, and pepper. Beat, pour over pizza.
I cup sliced sausage or crumbled bacon	
6 small eggs	**4.** Toss on herbs for color and flavor.
$\frac{1}{2}$ cup milk	**5.** Bake at 350 degrees for 13 minutes or until done. Cut into squares.
salt and pepper	
fresh chopped parsley or any herb	

Directions: Use the recipe and directions for biscuit pizza to solve the word problems. Show your work.

1. Layton wants to make biscuit pizzas for his Boy Scout troop. He needs to make a double batch to feed everyone. Eggs are $1.86 per dozen. How much will it cost Layton to buy enough eggs to make biscuit pizzas for his whole troop? _____

2. If I pound of bacon makes 2 cups of crumbled bacon, how much bacon will be needed to make a triple batch of biscuit pizzas? _____

3. If I recipe of biscuit pizza will feed 6 hungry kids, how many cups of cheese will be needed to make enough pizza to feed 36 kids? _____

4. If it takes Anna Maria 22 minutes to make a pizza and 13 minutes to bake it, what time should she start dinner if she wants to serve piping-hot pizza at 7:15 P.M.? _____

5. In order to triple the recipe, how many cups of fresh vegetables (peppers, tomatoes, and onions) will be needed? _____

0-7424-1815-4 *Numbers & Operations*

Name _____   Date _____

Multiplication Table

Directions: To master the multiplication table, fill in the blanks. Then study the table. Note that many facts are listed twice. If you know 7 x 6, you also know 6 x 7.

1	1	2	3	4	5	6	7	8	9	10	11	12
2		4	6	8	10	12	14	16	18	20	22	24
3			9	12	15	18	21	24	27	30	33	36
4				16	20	24	28	32	36	40	44	48
5					25	30	35	40	45	50	55	60
6						36	42	48	54	60	66	72
7							49	56	63	70	77	84
8								64	72	80	88	96
9									81	90	99	108
10										100	110	120
11											121	132
12												144

0-7424-1815-4 *Numbers & Operations*

Name _____ Date _____

Checking the Facts

Directions: Use the check chart to list and write an addition, multiplication, and division equation. Use the two numbers indicated. The first one has been done for you.

equations	1	2	3	4	5	6	8	9	10	12	15
1. 4 + 1 = 5 4 x 1 = 4 4 ÷ 1 = 4	✓			✓							
2.		✓					✓				
3.			✓				✓				
4.			✓					✓			
5.					✓				✓		
6.		✓							✓		
7.			✓							✓	
8.			✓								✓
9.						✓				✓	
10.					✓						✓

0-7424-1815-4 *Numbers & Operations*

Name _____ Date _____

Finding Multiplication Facts

Directions: Circle sets of 3 numbers that represent the 2 factors and the product of a multiplication equation. The equations may be hidden across, down, or diagonally. One has been done for you.

2	4	9	5	6	30	2	7	14	3	6	18	2
x												
5	3	15	6	1	6	7	6	42	9	9	81	1
=												
10	12	6	30	6	5	36	42	3	27	7	27	2
8	2	16	2	4	8	8	64	9	8	72	6	8
80	24	3	3	9	40	1	4	4	2	8	4	16
2	5	10	6	60	48	8	8	64	16	18	24	3
7	9	63	18	4	8	32	8	8	9	5	45	9
14	45	9	8	72	24	5	64	3	3	9	27	27
9	8	7	81	7	7	49	40	24	27	11	81	5
1	1	63	5	9	45	8	4	4	16	99	8	9
9	8	72	7	35	6	6	36	8	5	40	4	5
1	8	8	35	8	6	48	7	32	5	20	32	45

Do More: Create a hidden-number puzzle with division equations across, down, and diagonally.

0-7424-1815-4 *Numbers & Operations*

Name _____ Date _____

The Sum of It All

Directions: Use a calculator to find the sum of all the digits from 1 to 100. Begin by adding across, finding the sum of each row. Then add down, finding the grand total of all the sums.

1 + 2 + 3 + 4 + 5 + 6 + 7 + 8 + 9 + 10 = _____

11 + 12 + 13 + 14 + 15 + 16 + 17 + 18 + 19 + 20 = _____

21 + 22 + 23 + 24 + 25 + 26 + 27 + 28 + 29 + 30 = _____

31 + 32 + 33 + 34 + 35 + 36 + 37 + 38 + 39 + 40 = _____

41 + 42 + 43 + 44 + 45 + 46 + 47 + 48 + 49 + 50 = _____

51 + 52 + 53 + 54 + 55 + 56 + 57 + 58 + 59 + 60 = _____

61 + 62 + 63 + 64 + 65 + 66 + 67 + 68 + 69 + 70 = _____

71 + 72 + 73 + 74 + 75 + 76 + 77 + 78 + 79 + 80 = _____

81 + 82 + 83 + 84 + 85 + 86 + 87 + 88 + 89 + 90 = _____

91 + 92 + 93 + 94 + 95 + 96 + 97 + 98 + 99 + 100 = _____

Grand Total _____

Do More: Can you think of a better way to group the numbers to find the total more quickly? There is a simple way. Explain your idea on the back of this paper.

0-7424-1815-4 *Numbers & Operations*

Name _____ Date _____

Multiplying Mice 🐭

Directions: Marco loves animals—especially rodents. On the first day of January, he bought 2 mice. A month later, those 2 mice had turned into 8. And a month later, he counted 32 mice. On the average, each mouse was giving birth to 3 babies each month. Calculate and complete the chart to show how many mice Marco had at the beginning of each month. Use the data to solve the problems.

	New Mice	**Old Mice**	**Total Mice**
January	2		2
February	6	2	8
March	24	8	32
April	96	32	128
May			
June			
July			
August			
September			
October			
November			
December			

1. In June, will Marco have more or less than 1,000 mice? _____

2. Which month will Marco go over 1,000,000 mice? _____

3. Round off to thousands the number of mice Marco will have in July. _____

4. In December, how many mice will Marco have? _____

0-7424-1815-4 *Numbers & Operations*

Name _____ Date _____

Daily Double

Directions: Pretend that you won a prize. You don't know the amount of the prize, but you do know that you will get it in daily installments. The first day of February you get 1 penny. The second day you get 2 pennies, and so on, doubling the previous day's amount until the end of the month. Use your calculator to help you fill out the amount you will get every day. Before you begin, guess how much money you will receive on the last day of the month. Use your completed calendar to answer the questions on page 75.

February

1	2	3	4	5	6	7
8	9	10	11	12	13	14
15	16	17	18	19	20	21
22	23	24	25	26	27	28

0-7424-1815-4 *Numbers & Operations*

Name _____ Date _____

Daily Double

Directions: To solve the problems on this page, use the calendar on page 74.

1. Before you completed the calendar, did you think the prize would be a very big one? _____

2. Before you completed the calendar, how much did you estimate that you would receive on the last day? _____

3. Which day of the month did you receive more than $100? _____

4. What was the total prize money earned the first 7 days? _____

5. What was the total prize money received the last 3 days of the month? _____

6. If the contest had taken place on a leap year, how much would the last day's prize have been? _____

7. Which day of the month did you first receive more than $10,000? _____

8. Which 2 days of the month had a combined winnings of $7,864.32? _____

9. Which day of the month did you first receive more than $1,000,000? _____

10. What was the total prize money earned the second week? _____

0-7424-1815-4 *Numbers & Operations*

Check Your Skills—Operations

1. The commutative property of addition states that the order of the addends does not change the _____.

2. The associative property of addition means that the way addends are _____ does not change the sum.

3. Factors are the numbers _____ to get a product.

4. What are the factors in 3 × 4 = 12? _____

5. The commutative property of multiplication means that the _____ of the _____ does not change the product.

6. Write this equation as a multiplication problem: 9 + 9 + 9 + 9 + 9 = _____

7. Write an addition, multiplication, and division equation for this figure.

   _____

   _____

   _____

8. Use an exponent to write the number represented by this figure.

   _____

9. If 5 hens can lay 25 eggs per week, how long will it take 10 hens to lay 100 eggs? Which operation did you choose? Show your work. _____

10. Write out the 8 times table facts. _____

   _____

Name _____ Date _____

A Quick Way to Solve Problems

When multiplying or dividing numbers with numerous zeros at the end, you can temporarily remove all the zeros before multiplying or dividing. Then just add the zeros back onto the answer.

Example: 300 x 500 = 3 x 5 (15) plus 4 zeros (150,000).

Directions: Study the example. Then find the product or quotient for each problem below.

1. 10,000,000 x 8 = _____

2. 100,000 x 5 = _____

3. 10,000,000 ÷ 2 = _____

4. 300,000,000 ÷ 5 = _____

5. 1,000,000 x 11 = _____

6. 400,000,000 x 8 = _____

7. 10,000,000 x 89 = _____

8. 100,000 x 55 = _____

9. 10,000,000 ÷ 20 = _____

10. 100,000 ÷ 10 = _____

Do More: Estimate the total number students attending your school. Example: If there are 10 rooms and about 20 students per room, you might guess there are 200 students. After you estimate, ask the school principal for the actual figure. How accurate was your estimation?

0-7424-1815-4 *Numbers & Operations*

Name _____ Date _____

Adding Decimals

Directions: Rewrite the problem and align the decimal points. Use zeros as placeholders. Estimate first. Then find the sums. The first one has been started for you.

	Actual		**Estimation**

1. 613.91 + 47.1 =

    613.91 = 614   600 + 14
    + 047.10 = 47   + 50 − 3
    _____   _____
                     650 + 11 = 661

2. 293.2 + 69.99 =

3. 16.33 + 19.4 =

4. 0.79 + 29.11 + 19.99 =

5. 1.99 + 177.19 + 99.99 =

6. 28 + 80.14 + 96.62 =

7. 8.15 + 66.98 + 122.2 =

8. 911.9 + 5 + 643.11 =

78

Name _____   Date _____

The Fundraiser

A **decimal point** separates ones from tenths. It also is used to separate dollars from cents. The students at Southview School held a fundraiser for a new ping-pong table. The following chart shows how much each student in Room 5 raised in 1 month.

$

Barbara	$19.55	Fred	$120.44
Sarah	$25.72	Thomas	$239.57
Luis	$3.90	Chi Fa	$1,000.00

$

Directions: When adding dollars and cents, begin by lining up the decimal points. Estimate first. Then find the sums. Show your work for each of the word problems. The first one has been started for you.

		Actual	**Estimation**
1.	All together, how much did Barbara and Chi Fa raise?	$19.55	$20.00
		$1,000.00	$1,000.00

2. All together, how much did Thomas and Luis raise?

3. All together, how much did the 2 top fundraisers contribute?

4. What is the difference between the largest contribution and the smallest contribution?

5. All together, how much did the 2 girls raise?

Do More: If on the average, these 6 people can collect approximately the same amount each month, how much could they raise in 1 year?

0-7424-1815-4 *Numbers & Operations*

Subtracting Decimals

Directions: When subtracting decimals, as in addition, align the decimal points and insert zeros as placeholders. Estimate first. Then find the differences.

	Actual		**Estimation**

1. $56.89 - 11.02 =$

$$\begin{array}{r} 56.89 \\ - \ 11.02 \\ \hline \end{array}$$ = $$\begin{array}{r} 57 \\ 11 \\ \hline \end{array}$$ $$\begin{array}{r} 50 + 7 \\ - \ 10 + 1 \\ \hline 40 + 6 \ = \ 46 \end{array}$$

2. $89.30 - 1.201 =$

$$\begin{array}{r} 89.300 \\ - \ 1.201 \\ \hline \end{array}$$

3. $1.678 - 0.199 =$

4. $855.01 - 0.456 =$

Directions: Show your work as you solve each word problem.

5. Robert left for the mall with $19.50 in his wallet. After he bought a CD for $9.99, he ate a hamburger and fries that cost $3.45. Does Robert have enough left to buy a book that costs $2.19?

6. On Mother's Day, Marsha bought her mom a dozen roses and a card. The roses cost $21.50 and the card was $1.95. Marsha paid with two $20 bills. How much change did she get?

7. Francisco used a $20 bill to buy school lunch tickets for 1 week. The tickets cost $2.25 per day. How much change did Francisco get?

80

Name _____ Date _____

Sums and Differences of Like Fractions

Directions: When adding or subtracting like fractions, find the sum or difference of the numerators. The denominators do not change. Remember, the denominator tells you how many parts are in the whole. The numerator tells you how many parts out of the whole. For each addition problem, use the circle to prove your answer. Simplify when you can.

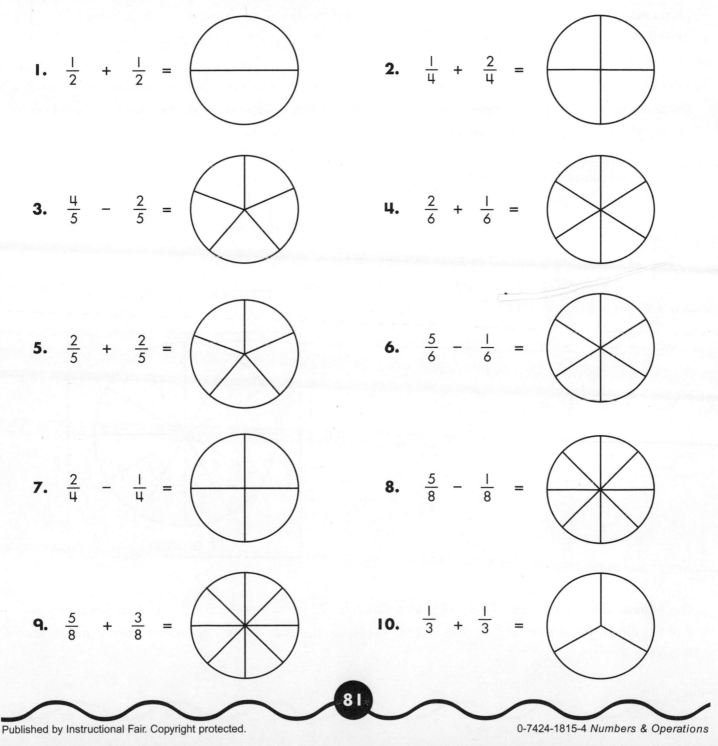

1. $\frac{1}{2} + \frac{1}{2} =$

2. $\frac{1}{4} + \frac{2}{4} =$

3. $\frac{4}{5} - \frac{2}{5} =$

4. $\frac{2}{6} + \frac{1}{6} =$

5. $\frac{2}{5} + \frac{2}{5} =$

6. $\frac{5}{6} - \frac{1}{6} =$

7. $\frac{2}{4} - \frac{1}{4} =$

8. $\frac{5}{8} - \frac{1}{8} =$

9. $\frac{5}{8} + \frac{3}{8} =$

10. $\frac{1}{3} + \frac{1}{3} =$

0-7424-1815-4 *Numbers & Operations*

Name _____   Date _____

Simplifying Improper Fractions

Improper fractions are fractions in which the numerator is greater than or equal to the denominator.

     Example: $\frac{6}{5}$ is an improper fraction.

Mixed numbers include both whole numbers and fractions. To express $\frac{6}{5}$ as a mixed number, write how many wholes and how many fractional parts are left over.

     Example: $\frac{6}{5} = 1\frac{1}{5}$

Directions: An orange has been cut in half. Each half has 6 sections. Each section represents $\frac{1}{12}$ of the whole orange. Use this information to answer the questions. Show your work.

1. A recipe calls for 24 sections of orange. How many oranges will be needed? _____

2. At recess, Larry ate 20 orange sections. At lunch he ate another 12. All together, how many oranges did Larry eat? _____

3. $\frac{5}{12} + \frac{9}{12} =$ _____

4. $\frac{8}{12} + \frac{10}{12} =$ _____

5. $\frac{7}{12} + \frac{9}{12} =$ _____

6. $\frac{11}{12} + \frac{9}{12} =$ _____

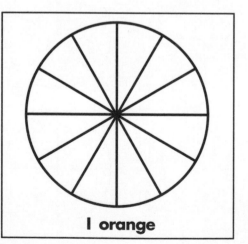

1 orange

Do More: One foot equals 12 inches, so an inch is $\frac{1}{12}$ of a foot. Make a paper airplane. Fly it. Measure how far it went in feet and inches. Write the distance as an improper fraction and as a mixed number.

82

Mixed Number Sums

Mixed numbers are numbers written as a whole number and a fraction.

      Example: $3\frac{1}{3}$

Directions: Color the pie slices different colors to solve the problem.

1.

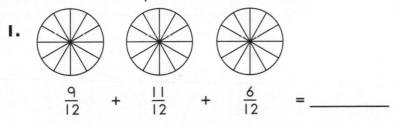

    $\frac{9}{12}$ + $\frac{11}{12}$ + $\frac{6}{12}$ = _____

2.   Another way to find the mixed number without drawing a picture is to find the sum of the numerators and divide by the denominator. To express the result as a mixed number, write the whole number. Then write the remainder as the fraction.

    a. $9 + 11 + 6 =$ _____

    b. _____ $\div 12 =$ _____ R _____ = _____

Directions: Find the sums of the fractions. Write them as a mixed numbers.

3. $\frac{1}{2} + \frac{3}{2} =$ 4. $\frac{3}{4} + \frac{3}{4} =$

5. $\frac{4}{6} + \frac{3}{6} =$ 6. $\frac{5}{8} + \frac{7}{8} =$

7. $\frac{1}{3} + \frac{5}{3} =$ 8. $\frac{5}{6} + \frac{4}{6} =$

9. $\frac{4}{5} + \frac{3}{5} =$ 10. $\frac{9}{12} + \frac{7}{12} =$

Do More: There are 12 months in 1 year. A month represents $\frac{1}{12}$ of a year. Write your approximate age as a mixed number.

     0-7424-1815-4 *Numbers & Operations*

Name _____ Date _____

Subtracting Unlike Fractions

When subtracting fractions with unlike denominators, you must first find the **least common denominator** (the number that both denominators will evenly divide into).

Example: $\dfrac{1}{3} = \dfrac{(1 \times 4)}{(3 \times 4)} = \dfrac{4}{12}$ $\dfrac{1}{4} = \dfrac{(1 \times 3)}{(4 \times 3)} = \dfrac{3}{12}$ $\dfrac{4}{12} - \dfrac{3}{12} = \dfrac{1}{12}$

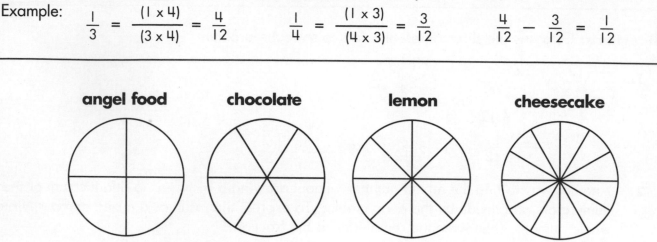

angel food   **chocolate**   **lemon**   **cheesecake**

Directions: Study the example. Then use the fractional sizes of the pies to write and solve the problems. Show your work.

1.   How much larger is a piece of angel food cake than chocolate cake?

2.   How much larger is a piece of chocolate cake than cheesecake?

3.   How much larger is a piece of lemon cake than cheesecake?

4.   How much larger is a piece of angel food cake than cheesecake?

5.   How much larger is a piece of angel food cake than lemon?

Do More: Here is a riddle to solve. When is it possible to multiply a number and get a product smaller than the factor?

84

Name _____ Date _____

Adding and Subtracting Unlike Fractions

> Remember, the **least common denominator** is the least common multiple of the denominators of two or more fractions.
>
> Example: For $\frac{1}{3}$ and $\frac{1}{4}$, 12 is the least common denominator.

Directions: Least common denominators are needed when adding and subtracting fractions. Find the least common denominator for each of the number pairs. Then find the sums or differences and simplifly to lowest terms. The first one has been started for you.

1. $\frac{1}{4} + \frac{3}{6} = \frac{}{12} + \frac{}{12} =$

2. $\frac{1}{2} - \frac{4}{9} =$

3. $\frac{4}{5} + \frac{1}{6} =$

4. $\frac{1}{10} + \frac{3}{3} =$

5. $\frac{2}{3} + \frac{3}{7} =$

6. $\frac{3}{4} - \frac{1}{3} =$

7. $\frac{1}{3} + \frac{3}{8} =$

8. $\frac{1}{7} + \frac{3}{3} =$

9. $\frac{4}{5} + \frac{1}{6} =$

10. $\frac{1}{2} + \frac{2}{5} =$

Published by Instructional Fair. Copyright protected. 0-7424-1815-4 *Numbers & Operations*

Name _____ Date _____

Fraction Subtraction

Directions: Find the differences. Begin by renaming the fractions so that they have the same denominator. To rename, find the least common denominator. Next write equivalent fractions using the least common denominator. Then you are ready to subtract.

1. $\dfrac{1}{2} - \dfrac{1}{3} =$

2. $\dfrac{1}{4} - \dfrac{1}{8} =$

3. $\dfrac{1}{3} - \dfrac{1}{6} =$

4. $\dfrac{1}{3} - \dfrac{1}{4} =$

5. $\dfrac{1}{2} - \dfrac{1}{4} =$

6. $\dfrac{1}{2} - \dfrac{1}{8} =$

7. $\dfrac{2}{5} - \dfrac{1}{3} =$

8. $\dfrac{3}{4} - \dfrac{3}{8} =$

Directions: Draw pictures to help you solve the problems.

9. Leon brought $\dfrac{1}{2}$ of a sandwich to school for lunch. His friend, Stan, forgot his lunch. So Leon gave $\dfrac{1}{3}$ of his sandwich to Stan. How much sandwich did Leon eat?

10. Babon had $\dfrac{1}{4}$ pound of chocolates. He gave $\dfrac{1}{2}$ to his friend. How much chocolate did Babon have left?

11. Kate earns $3.00 per half-hour for baby-sitting. How much does she earn in 15 minutes?

12. Nathan mowed $\dfrac{1}{2}$ of the backyard. His sister mowed $\dfrac{1}{4}$ of what hadn't been mowed. How much of the lawn is still unmowed?

0-7424-1815-4 *Numbers & Operations*

Name _____ Date _____

Multiplying Fractions

When multiplying fractions, begin by multiplying the numerators. Then multiply the denominators. Simplify if possible.

Example: $\frac{3}{4} \times \frac{4}{5} = \frac{12}{20}$ (divide by 4) $= \frac{3}{5}$

Reciprocals are two fractions whose product is 1.

Example: $\frac{3}{5} \times \frac{5}{3} = 1$

Directions: Study the example. Then find the products. Simplify your answers. Draw a picture to prove each answer.

1. $\frac{1}{2} \times \frac{4}{5} =$

2. $\frac{1}{4} \times \frac{4}{5} =$

3. $\frac{1}{3} \times \frac{3}{4} =$

4. $\frac{1}{5} \times \frac{5}{6} =$

5. $\frac{3}{5} \times \frac{1}{3} =$

6. $\frac{2}{3} \times \frac{6}{8} =$

7. $\frac{1}{6} \times \frac{3}{6} =$

8. $\frac{1}{8} \times \frac{4}{5} =$

9. $\frac{4}{7} \times \frac{1}{2} =$

10. $\frac{3}{4} \times \frac{2}{12} =$

Do More: Find a friend. Compare the pictures you drew to prove your answers. Were your pictures the same or different? Can you think of another way to prove the problem than the one you drew?

0-7424-1815-4 *Numbers & Operations*

Name _____ Date _____

Dividing Fractions

Directions: Study the example. Then find the quotients. Simplify to lowest terms. Show your work.

To divide fractions, multiply by the reciprocal of the divisor. The **divisor** is the second number in a division sentence (**dividend ÷ divisor = quotient**). **Reciprocals** are two fractions whose product is 1. The reciprocal of $\frac{3}{4}$ is $\frac{4}{3}$ because $\frac{3}{4} \times \frac{4}{3} = 1$.

Example: $\frac{1}{2} \div \frac{3}{4}$ (take the reciprocal of $\frac{3}{4}$, which is $\frac{4}{3}$) $\frac{1}{2} \times \frac{4}{3} = \frac{4}{6} = \frac{2}{3}$

To divide by whole or mixed numbers, convert them to improper fractions first.

Example: $\frac{1}{2} \div 1 = \frac{1}{2} \div \frac{5}{1} = \frac{1}{2} \times \frac{1}{5} = \frac{1}{10}$

$\frac{1}{2} \div 1\frac{1}{4} = \frac{1}{2} \div \frac{5}{4} = \frac{1}{2} \times \frac{4}{5} = \frac{4}{10}$

1. $\frac{2}{3} \div \frac{1}{2} =$

2. $\frac{1}{4} \div \frac{1}{3} =$

3. $\frac{1}{4} \div \frac{5}{8} =$

4. $\frac{1}{4} \div \frac{3}{5} =$

5. $\frac{2}{3} \div \frac{1}{2} =$

6. $\frac{1}{4} \div \frac{1}{4} =$

7. $\frac{1}{6} \div \frac{5}{8} =$

8. $\frac{3}{5} \div \frac{1}{7} =$

9. $\frac{3}{5} \div 5 =$

10. $\frac{3}{5} \div 2\frac{1}{2} =$

11. $\frac{1}{8} \div 2\frac{1}{2} =$

12. $\frac{1}{8} \div 8 =$

0-7424-1815-4 *Numbers & Operations*

Adding and Subtracting Integers

You can add and subtract integers using a number line. To **add integers**, pretend you are walking on a number line. Walk forward for positive numbers and backward for negative numbers.

$^-3 + {}^+4 = {}^+1$

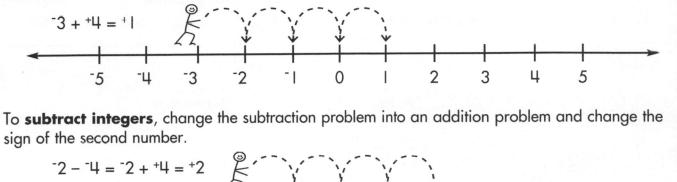

To **subtract integers**, change the subtraction problem into an addition problem and change the sign of the second number.

$^-2 - {}^-4 = {}^-2 + {}^+4 = {}^+2$

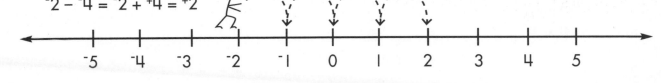

Directions: Solve the problems. Use the number line to help you.

1. $^-6 + {}^+3 =$

2. $^-3 - {}^-9 =$

3. $^-5 + {}^+1 =$

4. $^-8 - {}^-1 =$

5. $^-4 + {}^-2 =$

6. $^-8 - {}^+6 =$

7. $^-3 + {}^+3 =$

8. $^-7 - {}^-4 =$

9. $^-1 + {}^-5 =$

10. $^-11 - {}^+2 =$

11. $^-4 + {}^+2 =$

12. $^+8 - {}^-1 =$

Do More: To play this game, you will need a friend and a pair of dice. Take turns rolling the dice. The smaller number stands for a negative number and the larger number stands for is a positive number. (If the numbers are the same, pretend they are both positive.) Find and keep track of the sums. The person with the highest score at the end of 12 rolls is the winner.

     0-7424-1815-4 Numbers & Operations

Name _____   Date _____

Multiplying Integers

Rules:
1. When multiplying **two positive** numbers, the product is **positive**.
2. When multiplying **two negative** numbers, the product is also **positive**.
3. When multiplying **a negative and a positive** number, the product is always **negative**.

Directions: Estimate first. Then find the products. Show your work.

	Actual	**Estimation**

1. ⁻3 x ⁺5 =   _____

2. ⁻7 x ⁻8 =   _____

3. ⁻10 x ⁺50 =   _____

4. ⁻717 x ⁻3 =   _____

5. ⁺309 x ⁺34 =   _____

6. ⁻909 x ⁺80 =   _____

7. ⁺311 x ⁻59 =   _____

8. ⁻7.88 x ⁻8 =   _____

9. ⁻98.1 x ⁺5.2 =   _____

10. ⁻0.5 x ⁻855 =   _____

0-7424-1815-4 *Numbers & Operations*

Name _____ Date _____

Dividing Integers

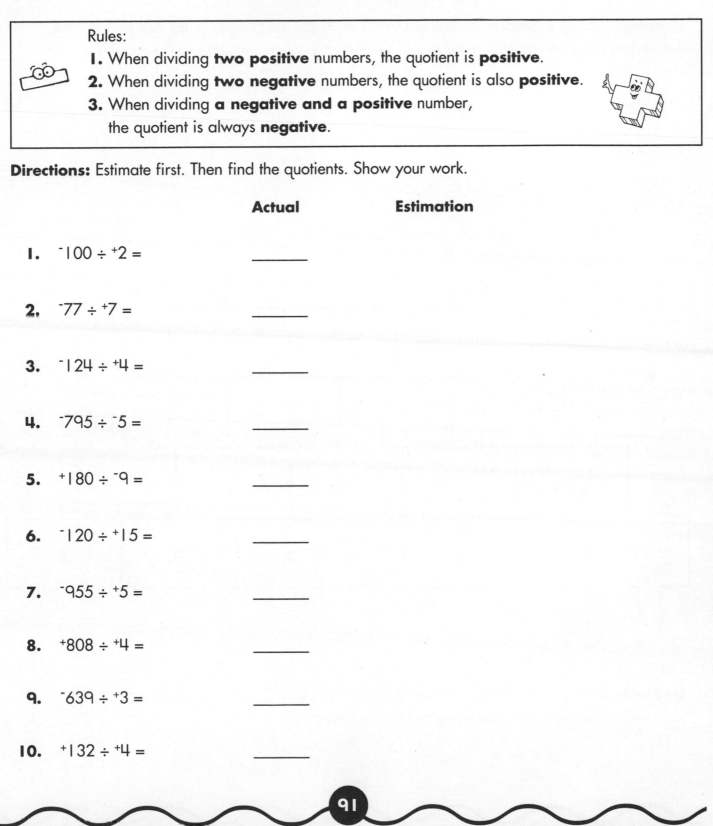

Rules:
1. When dividing **two positive** numbers, the quotient is **positive**.
2. When dividing **two negative** numbers, the quotient is also **positive**.
3. When dividing **a negative and a positive** number, the quotient is always **negative**.

Directions: Estimate first. Then find the quotients. Show your work.

	Actual	Estimation
1. ⁻100 ÷ ⁺2 =	_____	
2. ⁻77 ÷ ⁺7 =	_____	
3. ⁻124 ÷ ⁺4 =	_____	
4. ⁻795 ÷ ⁻5 =	_____	
5. ⁺180 ÷ ⁻9 =	_____	
6. ⁻120 ÷ ⁺15 =	_____	
7. ⁻955 ÷ ⁺5 =	_____	
8. ⁺808 ÷ ⁺4 =	_____	
9. ⁻639 ÷ ⁺3 =	_____	
10. ⁺132 ÷ ⁺4 =	_____	

0-7424-1815-4 *Numbers & Operations*

Name _____ Date _____

Climbing the Multiplication Pyramid

Directions: Multiply numbers in adjacent boxes and write the product in the box above them. Before you begin, guess what number will be at the top when you have completed the pyramid climb. Write it here: _____

Do More: There is a mathematical rule called the "property of zero." Can you guess what it is? If you don't know, find out what it means.

0-7424-1815-4 *Numbers & Operations*

Name _____ Date _____

Long Division Practice

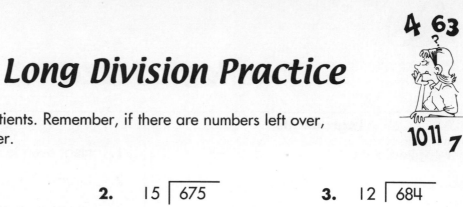

Directions: Find the quotients. Remember, if there are numbers left over, show them as a remainder.

1. 50 ⟌655

2. 15 ⟌675

3. 12 ⟌684

4. 43 ⟌459

5. 42 ⟌949

6. 33 ⟌489

7. 66 ⟌768

8. 72 ⟌849

9. 45 ⟌855

10. 31 ⟌609

11. 22 ⟌250

12. 64 ⟌878

0-7424-1815-4 *Numbers & Operations*

Name _____ Date _____

Magic Pizza

Ingredients	Directions
Crust Ingredients 2 tablespoons Parmesan cheese 1 cup of milk 2 large eggs $\frac{1}{2}$ cup of biscuit mix **Topping Ingredients** $\frac{1}{2}$ cup pizza sauce 1 cup cooked sausage or ground beef $\frac{1}{4}$ cup chopped onions $\frac{1}{4}$ cup chopped bell peppers 2 tablespoons Parmesan cheese 1 cup shredded mozzarella cheese	1. Heat oven to 425 degrees. 2. Grease 1 pie plate per 4 servings. 3. Sprinkle onion and Parmesan cheese in pie plate. 4. Beat milk, eggs, and biscuit mix for 15 seconds in blender on high. 5. Pour into pie plate. 6. Bake 20 minutes. 7. Remove from oven and spread pizza sauce over top. 8. Top with remaining ingredients. 9. Bake 12 minutes, until cheese is light brown. 10. Cool 5 minutes. Enjoy!

Directions: Use the recipe and directions for pizza to solve the word problems on this page and page 95. Show your work.

1. To make 3 pizzas, how many cups of fresh vegetables (onions and bell peppers) will be needed?

2. If Mrs. Jobesmith wants to make 4 pizzas for her Girl Scout troop, how many cups of biscuit mix will she need?

3. If you need to bake 24 pizzas, how much of each kind of cheese will you need? (16 tablespoons = 1 cup)

4. If ground beef cooks down to 50% of its original size, how much raw hamburger is needed to make 20 pizzas?

94

Name _____ Date _____

Magic Pizza

Directions: Use the recipe on page 94 to answer the questions.

1. There are 16 tablespoons in 1 cup. What percent of the cheese used on 1 magic pizza is Parmesan?

2. How many cups of pizza sauce is needed to make a dozen pizzas?

3. If 2 large eggs equal $\frac{1}{4}$ cup, label the pizza to show the fractional part of each ingredient.

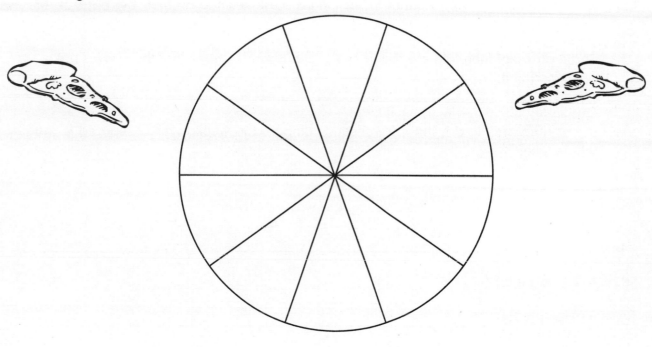

Do More: Try the pizza recipe at home.

Published by Instructional Fair. Copyright protected.

0-7424-1815-4 *Numbers & Operations*

Name _____ Date _____

Ratio

A **ratio** is the comparison of 2 numbers.

> Example: 2:5 might mean that 2 out of 5 people prefer tea to coffee.
>
> There are 3 ways to write a ratio: 2 to 5 , $\frac{2}{5}$, or 2:5.
>
> When both terms of a ratio are multiplied or divided by the same number (other than 0), the result is an **equivalent ratio**.
>
> Example: Take the ratio 2 to 5.
>   Multiply both terms by 5. (2 x 5 = 10 and 5 x 5 = 25)
>   10 to 25 is equivalent to 2 to 5.

Directions: Write a ratio for each story problem.

1. In troop number 112, 9 out of 10 of the boys use ketchup on their big bags of 48 fries.

2. Three different men told me that 4 out of 5 husbands prefer that their wives not wear perfume.

3. What ratio are the days in the weekend compared to weekdays? Compared to the whole week?

Directions: Are these ratios equivalent? Explain why or why not.

4. 5:8 and 15:24 _____

5. 4:12 and 12:36 _____

6. 1:5 and 5:20 _____

Directions: What number makes these ratios equivalent? Fill in the missing numbers.

7. 15 to 5 and 3: _____   8. 4:16 and 8: _____   9. $\frac{9}{10}$ and 45: _____

0-7424-1815-4 *Numbers & Operations*

Name _____ Date _____

Percents and Ratios

Number out of Ten	Percent	Decimal	Ratio
10	100%	1.00	10:10
9	90%	0.9	9:10
8	80%	0.8	8:10
7	70%	0.7	7:10
6	60%	0.6	6:10
5	50%	0.5	5:10
4	40%	0.4	4:10
3	30%	0.3	3:10
2	20%	0.2	2:10
1	10%	0.1	1:10

Directions: Use the chart to help you solve the word problems.

1. If 90% of a class of 10 can multiply, how many students in the class cannot multiply?
_____

2. If 70% of a class of 10 likes chocolate pudding, how many students don't like chocolate pudding? _____

3. If 10% of a scout troop of 10 cannot tie knots, what ratio of scouts can tie knots? _____

4. If 50% of a class of 20 is away on a field trip, how many students are still at school?
_____

5. If 100% of a class of 85 went to the puppet show, how many didn't go to the show?
_____

6. If 90% of a class of 10 wears braces, what ratio of kids do not wear braces? _____

Do More: Rick can paint a small room in 2 hours. His helper can paint the same room in 3 hours. If they each work 1 hour, what fraction of the room will be left unpainted?

0-7424-1815-4 *Numbers & Operations*

Name _____ Date _____

Percents, Fractions, and Decimals

Directions: Color each bar as indicated. Then answer the questions using the bars.

I. 10% red, 20% blue

What percent is colored? _____

What fraction is not colored? _____

What decimal is colored? _____

2. 80% green, 10% yellow

What percent is colored? _____

What fraction is colored? _____

What decimal is not colored? _____

3. 40% red, 10% black

What percent is not colored? _____

What fraction is colored? _____

What decimal is not colored? _____

4. 50% orange, 25% pink

What percent is not colored? _____

What fraction is not colored? _____

What decimal is colored? _____

5. 55% green, 15% blue

What percent is not colored? _____

What fraction is colored? _____

What decimal is colored? _____

6. 15% yellow, 85% pink

What percent is colored? _____

What fraction is not colored? _____

What decimal is colored? _____

7. 50% green, 45% blue

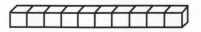

What percent is colored? _____

What fraction is not colored? _____

What decimal is not colored? _____

8. 10% red, 80% pink

What percent is not colored? _____

What fraction is colored? _____

What decimal is not colored? _____

0-7424-1815-4 *Numbers & Operations*

Counting Household Appliances

Appliance	Percentage of Households in the U.S.
Television (color)	98%
Television (black and white)	20%
Refrigerator	85%
Range	61%
Oven (regular)	91%
Microwave	84%
Dishwasher	45%
Washer	77%
Dryer	57%
Computer	97%

Directions: Use the chart to solve these word problems. Remember, a percent means how many out of 100. If you want to know how many in 200 households, the number must be doubled.

1. In 100 households, how many own color televisions? _____

2. In 500 households, how many own a microwave? _____

3. In 300 households, how many own a dishwasher? _____

4. In 50 households, how many own a black-and-white television? _____

5. In 25 households, how many own a black-and-white television? _____

6. In 1,000 households, how many own a computer? _____

7. In 500 households, how many own a dishwasher? _____

8. In 1,000 households, how many own a washer? _____

Do More: There are 3 lights in a room. The 3 switches to turn the lights off and on are in another room where you cannot see which switch turns on which light. You must figure out which switch belongs to which light, but you can only go into the room with the lights 1 time. What will you do?

0-7424-1815-4 *Numbers & Operations*

Name _____ Date _____

Is It Enough?

Directions: Answer the questions. Show your work.

Sun-Mi has been saving her money for a new pair of in-line skates. She has saved $85. The skates are regularly priced at $112. The store has them on sale for 20% off.

1. What percentage of the full price will the skates cost?

100% − 20% = _____

2. How much will the skates cost?

_____ × $112 = _____

3. Two days later, the skates are marked 30% off. How much will the skates cost now? _____

4. There is a 4% sales tax in Sun-Mi's state.

a. How much will the sales tax on the skates be (assuming they are still 30% off)? _____

b. Does Sun-Mi have enough money to buy the skates? Explain. _____

5. Sun-Mi's friend Jordan loves the in-line skates. He has $60 saved. How much more does Jordan need to buy the skates at 30% off before tax is added? _____

6. The 30% off sale only lasts another 3 weeks. Jordan needs 5 weeks to save enough money. In 5 weeks, the skates will be 15% off.

a. How much will the skates cost at 15% off? _____

b. How much will the tax be on the skates at 15% off (4% sales tax)? _____

Do More: Explain how to find the price of a $45 sweater that is on sale for 25% off.

0-7424-1815-4 *Numbers & Operations*

Name _____ Date _____

Papa's Burger Barn

Specials	Price List	
Wednesday—all burgers 33% off	Papa Burger	$3.00
Thursday—buy a burger, get $\frac{1}{2}$ off another burger	Mama Burger	$2.00
	Baby Burger	$1.00
Friday—fries half off	Fries	$1.50
Sunday—1 free soda with burger	Soda	$2.00

Directions: Use the Burger Barn specials and price list to solve the problems. Show your work.

1. On Wednesday, Melissa bought 4 Papa Burgers. How much was her bill?

2. On Thursday, Linda and her friend Amy were thirsty. They bought 6 sodas and 2 Papa Burgers. How much was their bill?

3. On Saturday, Mr. George bought each of the 9 boys on his ball team a bag of fries and a soda. If he had gone on Friday, how much money could he have saved?

4. On Monday, Max goes to Papa's Burger Barn with a $2.00-off coupon. He bought 2 Papa Burgers, fries, and a soda. How much was his bill?

5. On Sunday, Miller went to Papa's Burger Barn and ordered 3 sodas and 3 Papa Burgers. How much was his bill?

6. On Wednesday, Joshua took his little sister Meg to Papa's Burger Barn. He ordered a Papa Burger, a Baby Burger, 2 bags of fries, and 2 sodas. How much was his bill?

0-7424-1815-4 *Numbers & Operations*

Name _____   Date _____

Estimating Percentages

Directions: To estimate percentages, round off to the nearest tenth, then multiply. Before figuring each percentage, estimate and record your thinking. The first one has been started for you.

1. Bernice always saves 9% of her allowance. Last year her allowance was $5 per week. How much did she save?

   Estimate: Round 9% to 10%. $5 x 50 weeks = $250 x 0.10 = $25.00.
                 Since 9% is less than 10% the answer will be a little less than $25.00

   Solve: 9% = 0.09 x $5.00 x 52 weeks = _____

2. Jonathan's grandmother gave him $100 on each of his birthdays. He always saved 45% of his birthday money. When Jonathan was 12, how much had he saved?

   Estimate:

   Solve:

3. Thomasio inherited $3,000 from his grandfather. He put it in the bank and earned 9% interest. At the end of 3 years, how much interest had Thomasio earned? All together, how much did he have?

   Estimate:

   Solve:

4. Leo sold his dirt bike for $550. He put the money in the bank at 8%. After a year, how much interest had he earned? All together, how much did he have?

   Estimate:

   Solve:

0-7424-1815-4 *Numbers & Operations*

Name _____ Date _____

Interest

Interest is the amount of money paid for the use of money. It is a percent of the amount of money invested, borrowed, or loaned.

Principal is the money placed in a bank or borrowed.

Rate of interest is the percent earned or charged, usually per year. **Time** is how long the money is in the account or borrowed.

Example: 6% interest means that each month 0.5% (6% ÷ 12 months) is paid.

Directions: Use the interest formula **i = p x r x t** (interest = principal x rate x time) to complete the chart. Show your work. The first one has been started for you. Remember, 6 months = $\frac{1}{2}$ year or 0.5 year.

	Principal	Yearly Rate of Interest	Time	Interest	Total with Interest (Principal + Interest)
1.	$6,000	6% x 0.06	6 months (0.5 year)	= $180	= $6,180
2.	$500	3%	1 year		
3.	$1,000	10%	3 months (= _____ year)		
4.	$10,000	5%	2 years		
5.	$2,500	10%	20 years		

Published by Instructional Fair. Copyright protected.

0-7424-1815-4 *Numbers & Operations*

Estimating Products

Directions: Before multiplying, write your estimations by rounding off the numbers to the nearest ten or hundred. Then find the products. The first one has been started for you.

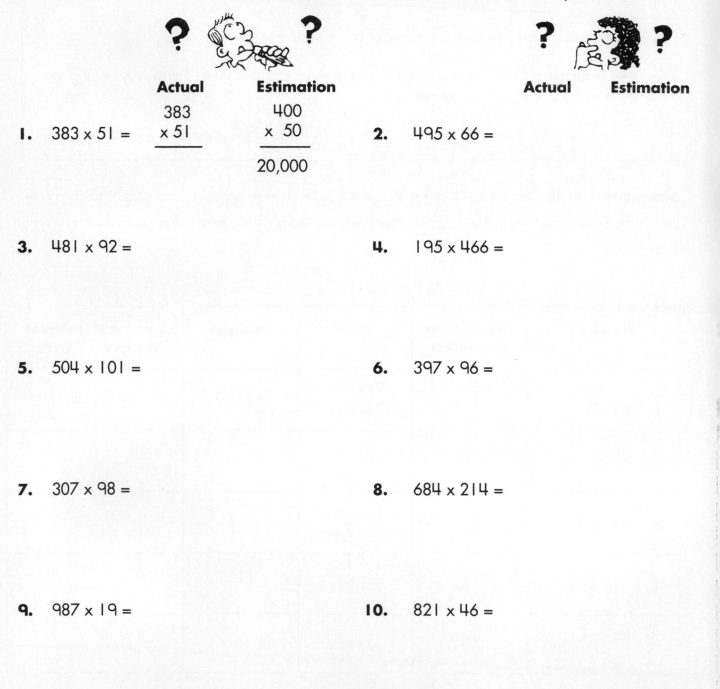

	Actual	**Estimation**
	383	400
1. 383 × 51 =	× 51	× 50
		20,000

2. 495 × 66 =

3. 481 × 92 =

4. 195 × 466 =

5. 504 × 101 =

6. 397 × 96 =

7. 307 × 98 =

8. 684 × 214 =

9. 987 × 19 =

10. 821 × 46 =

Published by Instructional Fair. Copyright protected.

0-7424-1815-4 *Numbers & Operations*

Name _____ Date _____

Estimating Quotients

Directions: Before multiplying, write your estimations by rounding off the numbers to the nearest ten or hundred. Then find the products. The first one has been started for you.

	Actual	Estimation		Actual	Estimation

1. $7{,}812 \div 93 = 93\overline{)7{,}812}^{\,84}$ $100\overline{)8{,}000}^{\,80}$

2. $4{,}410 \div 98 =$

3. $3{,}168 \div 88 =$

4. $8{,}811 \div 89 =$

5. $1{,}767 \div 19 =$

6. $2{,}695 \div 49 =$

7. $4{,}539 \div 51 =$

8. $1{,}122 \div 11 =$

9. $2{,}523 \div 29 =$

10. $8{,}670 \div 102 =$

0-7424-1815-4 *Numbers & Operations*

Parking Problems

Directions: Answer the questions. Show your work.

There are a total of 2,400 tires on vehicles in a parking lot.

1. What is the maximum number of each type of vehicle that could be parked in the lot?

    a. cars

    b. motorcycles

    c. 18-wheelers

2. If $\frac{1}{12}$ of the tires belong to motorcycles, how many motorcycles are parked there?

3. There are four 18-wheeler trucks in the parking lot. How many tires belong to trucks?

4. The remainder of the tires belong to cars, pickup trucks, minivans, and SUVs.

    a. How many of these vehicles are in the parking lot?

    b. If $\frac{1}{4}$ of the vehicles remaining are minivans, how many minivans are there?

    c. If $\frac{1}{2}$ of the vehicles remaining are cars, how many cars are there?

    d. If $\frac{1}{8}$ of the vehicles remaining are pickup trucks and $\frac{1}{8}$ are SUVs, how many pickup trucks and how many SUVs are there?

0-7424-1815-4 *Numbers & Operations*

Name _____ Date _____

Missing Numbers

Directions: Find the value of each shape.

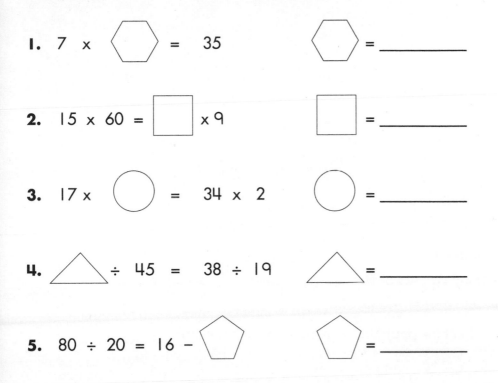

1. $7 \times$ ⬡ $= 35$ ⬡ = _____

2. $15 \times 60 =$ ▢ $\times 9$ ▢ = _____

3. $17 \times$ ◯ $= 34 \times 2$ ◯ = _____

4. △ $\div 45 = 38 \div 19$ △ = _____

5. $80 \div 20 = 16 -$ ⬠   ⬠ = _____

Directions: Find the numbers that make all three equations true. Shapes that are the same represent the same number. Shapes that are different represent different numbers.

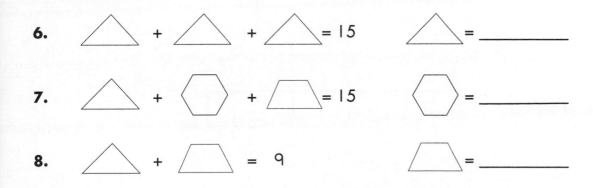

6. △ $+$ △ $+$ △ $= 15$ △ = _____

7. △ $+$ ⬡ $+$ ▱ $= 15$ ⬡ = _____

8. △ $+$ ▱ $= 9$ ▱ = _____

Do More: Explain the strategies you used to find your answers.

0-7424-1815-4 *Numbers & Operations*

Check Your Skills—Computation

1. $18.33 + 19.9 =$

2. $855.01 - 0.456 =$

3. $\dfrac{8}{12} + \dfrac{10}{12} =$

4. $\dfrac{3}{4} - \dfrac{1}{3} =$

5. $\dfrac{1}{5} \times \dfrac{5}{6} =$

6. $\dfrac{1}{4} \div \dfrac{1}{3} =$

7. $^-14 + ^-3 =$

8. $^-6 - ^-8 =$

9. $^-5 \times ^-855 =$

10. $3{,}038 \div 31 =$

11. Mrs. Silverstein wants to make 8 pizzas for her bridge club. The pizza recipe calls for $1\frac{1}{2}$ pounds of cheese, how many pounds of cheese will she need? Show your work. _____

12. If 25 girls out of 100 like to chew peppermint gum, what is that ratio? _____

13. If 25 boys out of 100 like to chew fruit-flavored gum, what decimal represents the fruit-flavored gum chewers? _____

14. If 9 out of 12 women won't chew gum, what is the fraction of women who will chew gum? _____

15. If 2 out of every 3 blondes have blue eyes, what percent of blondes have blue eyes? _____

16. Shade 70% of the bar.

    a. What percent is not shaded? _____

    b. What fraction is not shaded? _____

    c. What decimal is not shaded? _____

0-7424-1815-4 *Numbers & Operations*

Post Test

1. What is the absolute value of $^+9$? _____

2. Write seven hundred eighty-nine thousand four hundred three. _____

3. Round 67,091 to the nearest thousand. _____

4. **a.** Write 8,010,002 in expanded form.

   _____

   b. What is the value of the 1? _____

5. In 1,421.053, which numeral represents thousandths? _____

6. Complete the chart.

Decimal	Fraction	Percent
0.75		
		10%

7. What is the least common denominator of $\frac{1}{4}$ and $\frac{2}{3}$? _____

8. What is the least common multiple of 5 and 8? _____

9. What is the greatest common factor of 18 and 30? _____

10. Explain the commutative property of addition.

    _____

    _____

11. Explain the associative property of addition.

    _____

    _____

12. In $72 \div 9 = 8$, 72 is the _____, 9 is the _____, and 8 is the _____.

13. The way factors are grouped does not change the product. What property of multiplication is this? _____

0-7424-1815-4 *Numbers & Operations*

Post Test

Name _____   **Date** _____

14. Write this equation as a repeated addition problem: 8 x 4 = 32 _____

15. Write an addition, multiplication, and division equation for the figure to the right.

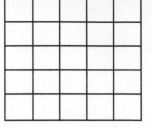

16. Use an exponent to write a number represented by this figure: _____

17. If 10 hens can lay 60 eggs per week, how long will it take 100 hens to lay 600 eggs? _____

18. If a cookie recipe calls for $\frac{1}{4}$ cup butter, how much butter will you need to make 12 batches of cookies? _____

19. $81.01 + 0.24 =$

20. $988.8 - 23.5 =$

21. $\frac{1}{8} + \frac{3}{8} =$

22. $\frac{1}{3} - \frac{1}{12} =$

23. $\frac{1}{4} \times \frac{4}{5} =$

24. $\frac{1}{8} \div \frac{1}{4} =$

25. $^-11 - ^-8 =$

26. $^-987 \times ^-11 =$

27. $^-501 + ^-12 =$

28. $713 - 568 =$

29. If Victoria owns 3 shirts, 4 pairs of jeans, and 1 hat, how many ways can she combine the clothes to make different outfits? _____

30. Complete the chart by writing the sum, difference, product, and quotient for each number pair.

	25, 20	100, 5	1,000,10
Sum			
Difference			
Product			
Quotient			

110

0-7424-1815-4 *Numbers & Operations*

Answer Key

1. 7
2. 9,700,092
3. 8,700,000
4. **a.** 9,000,000 + 900,000 + 1,000
   + 400 + 50
   b. 1,000
5. 9
6. **a.** 3 squares shaded,
   b. $\frac{7}{10}$ is not shaded
7. **a.** 0.5, $\frac{1}{2}$, 50%
   b. 0.01, $\frac{1}{100}$, 1%
8. 24
9. 12
10. 33
11. order
12. addends
13. product, factors
14. 5 × 6 = 30
15. 8 + 8 + 8 + 8 + 8 + 8 + 8 + 8 =
    64, 8 × 8 = 64, 64 ÷ 8 = 8
16. 1 week
17. $\frac{12}{3}$ = 4 cups
18. 32.13
19. 743.494
20. $\frac{16}{12}$ = 1 $\frac{4}{12}$ = 1 $\frac{1}{3}$
21. $\frac{1}{8}$
22. $\frac{3}{24}$ = $\frac{1}{8}$
23. $\frac{2}{3}$
24. ⁻17
25. ⁺1,728
26. ⁺1,573
27. 6 $\frac{3}{4}$ pounds
28. **a.** 2   **b.** 8

1. 4 × 10 = 40
2. 8 × 1,000,000 = 8,000,000
3. 2 × 10,000 = 20,000
4. 3 × 1,000 = 3,000
5. hundreds
6. hundred thousands
7. 8   8. 4
9. 9   10. 100,000

Do More: 3 (24,369,147)

1. Answers will vary.
2. **a.** hundred thousands
   b. ten thousands
   c. hundreds
3. $3,746,985.10
4. **a.** 9
   b. 5
   c. 4
5. **a.** hundred thousands
   b. millions
   c. tens
6. $3,046,985.10
7. $3,746,985.10
8. eleven million two hundred forty
   thousand nine hundred fifty-five
   dollars and thirty cents

1. 540,001   2. 830,750
3. 96,500   4. 317,059
5. 220,806   6. 835,570
7. 346,192   8. 592,752
9. 104,267   10. 506,048
11. 418,759   12. 329,742

1. 1,040,000   2. 1,000,000
3. 1,044,000   4. 43,512
5. thousands   6. 4 (1,044,000)
7. $10,000,000   8. $120,000,000

1. 31 million, 589 thousand,
   1 hundred, 53
2. 18 million, 723 thousand,
   9 hundred, 91
3. 18 million, 136 thousand, 81
4. 12 million, 71 thousand,
   8 hundred, 42
5. 31,589,000
6. 19,000,000
7. 18,000,000
8. 12,072,000

1. Answers may vary.
   a. 1,000 + 300 + 60
   b. one thousand, three hundred sixty
   c. 1 thousand, 360
2. Answers may vary.
   a. 50,000 + 6,000 + 700 + 80 + 1
   b. fifty-six thousand, seven hundred
   eighty-one
   c. 56 thousand, 7 hundred, 81
3. Answers will vary.

0-7424-1815-4 *Numbers & Operations*

Answer Key

Some possibilities:
30 + 6, thirty-six, 3 dozen.

4. **a.** ⁻6

   b. ⁻5

   c. 8,953

   d. 1,000

   e. 569 1/2 or 569.5

   f. 5,600,543

Representational Form 16

1. standard form: 4,321
   expanded form:
   4,000 + 300 + 20 + 1
   word form: four thousand
   three hundred twenty-one
   representational form:
   4 thousand cubes, 3 hundred
   flats, 2 ten rods, 1 one

2. standard form: 785
   expanded form: 700 + 80 + 5
   word form: seven hundred eighty-five
   representational form: 7 hundred
   flats, 8 ten rods, 5 ones

3. standard form: 5,010
   expanded form: 5,000 + 10
   word form: five thousand ten
   representational form: 5 thousand
   cubes, 1 ten rod

4. standard form: 8,072
   expanded form: 8,000 + 70 + 2
   word form: eight thousand seventy-two
   representational form: 8 thousand
   cubes, 7 ten rods, 2 ones

5. standard form: 12,011
   expanded form: 10,000 + 2,000 +
   10 + 1
   word form: twelve thousand eleven
   representational form: 12 thousand
   cubes, 1 ten rod, 1 one

The Same Number 17

1. expanded form:
   3,000 + 900 + 40
   short word form:
   3 thousand, 9 hundred, 40
   word form: three thousand nine
   hundred forty

2. expanded form:
   1,000 + 100 + 20 + 2
   short word form: 1 thousand,
   1 hundred, 22
   word form: one thousand
   one hundred twenty-two

3. expanded form: 1,000 + 900 + 60
   short word form: 1 thousand,
   9 hundred, 60
   word form: one thousand
   nine hundred sixty

4. expanded form: 4,000,000 +
   700,000 + 80,000 + 9,000 +
   400 + 50 + 6
   short word form: 4 million,
   789 thousand, 4 hundred, 56
   word form: four million seven
   hundred eighty-nine thousand
   four hundred fifty-six

What's Next? 18

1. 67,810; 67,812; 67,813
   a. 8
   b. 7
   c. 6

2. 7,001; 7,003; 7,004
   a. 7,000 + 4
   b. seven thousand three
   c. 7 thousand cubes, 1 one

3. 5,001,303; 5,001,304;
   5,001,306
   a. 5
   b. 1
   c. 0

4. 11,011; 11,012; 11,013
   a. 10,000 + 1,000 + 10 + 1
   b. eleven thousand eleven
   c. 11 thousand cubes, 1 ten rod,
   2 ones

5. 1,999; 2,000; 2,002
   a. 9
   b. 1
   c. 2

Number Charts 19

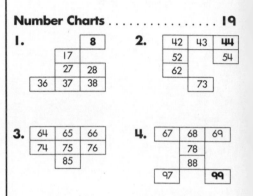

Moving Around the Number Charts . . 20

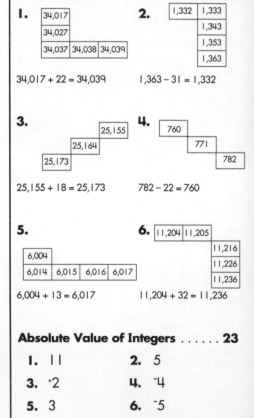

1. 34,017 + 22 = 34,039
2. 1,363 – 31 = 1,332
3. 25,155 + 18 = 25,173
4. 782 – 22 = 760
5. 6,004 + 13 = 6,017
6. 11,204 + 32 = 11,236

Absolute Value of Integers 23

1. 11
2. 5
3. ⁺2
4. ⁻4
5. 3
6. ⁻5

0-7424-1815-4 *Numbers & Operations*

Answer Key

7. ⁻2   **8.** neither

Do More: 9 jumps

Comparing Integers 22

1. =   **2.** >   **3.** >

4. <   **5.** =   **6.** <

7. <   **8.** =   **9.** <

10. a. ⁻4 $\frac{1}{2}$, ⁻0.5, ⁺1 $\frac{1}{2}$, ⁺5.5

   b. ⁻6, ⁻4, 0, ⁺3.5, ⁺4, ⁺5

Do More: ⁻25 and ⁺75

Ordering Integers 23

1. a. ⁻6.5, ⁻2.5, 0, ⁺2.5, ⁺3, ⁺3.5

   b. numbers correctly placed on
      number line

2. a. ⁺1, ⁺4, ⁻4.5, ⁺5.5, ⁻6, ⁺7

   b. absolute value: ⁺1, ⁺4, ⁻4.5, ⁻6, ⁺7
      as written: ⁻6, ⁻4.5, ⁺1, ⁺4, ⁺5.5, ⁺7

3. a. <   **b.** <   **c.** >

   d. <   **e.** <   **f.** >

4. a. <   **b.** <   **c.** >

   d. =   **e.** >   **f.** >

Do More: ⁺6 and ⁻6

Decimals 24

1. 0.2

2. 0.4

3. 0.16

4. 0.24

Do More: 0.001

Making Cents of It 25

1. 5 squares

2. 1 row

3. 2 rows

4. 1 row plus 3 squares

5. 3 rows plus 3 squares

6. 69¢   Do More: $\frac{1}{1,000}$

How Much Money? 26

1. no, need 11¢ more

2. yes, 8¢ change

3. no, need 47¢ more

4. yes, 5¢ change

5. no, need 5¢ more

Change, Please 27

1. $2.61   **2.** $2.18

3. $1.54   **4.** $2.55

5. $1.83   **6.** $2.39

7. $3.15   **8.** $3.20

In the Bank 28

Answers may vary.

One answer given.

1. 1 half-dollar, 3 dimes,
   1 nickel, 2 pennies

2. 2 quarters, 1 dime, 6 nickels,
   4 pennies

3. 3 half-dollars, 6 nickels,
   3 pennies

4. 6 nickels, 16 pennies

5. 8 dimes, 8 pennies

6. 3 half-dollars, 1 quarter,
   1 penny

7. 2 half-dollars, 18 dimes,
   4 pennies

8. 1 half-dollar, 2 quarters,
   2 pennies

Naming the Digits 29

1. 4   **2.** 8

3. 9   **4.** 6

5. 7   **6.** 5

7. 5 x 10,000 = 50,000

8. 1 x 1,000,000 = 1,000,000

9. 2 x 1 = 2

10. 8 x 0.001 = 0.008

Do More: hundred thousand (678,951.234)

Density of Population 30

1. 479.2

2. Pennsylvania

3. Texas

4. California, New York, Florida

5. Texas, Pennsylvania

6. New York, Florida, Pennsylvania

7. Texas and Pennsylvania

8. Florida

Comparing Decimals 31

1. <   **2.** <

3. <   **4.** <

5. <   **6.** <

7. >   **8.** >

9. <   **10.** <

11. 60 + 5 + 0.7 + 0.08

12. 90 + 4 + 0.1 + 0.03

13. 800 + 90 + 7 + 0.4 + 0.03
    + 0.001

14. 700 + 10 + 2 + 0.01

15. 10,000 + 1,000 + 300 + 1 + 0.01
    + 0.002

16. 8,000 + 0.1

17. 50 + 0.03

18. 400 + 20 + 2 + 0.02

19. 30,000 + 1,000 + 300 + 10 + 3
    + 0.01 + 0.003

20. 60,000 + 3,000 + 1 + 0.1 + 0.02

Rounding Decimals 32

1. 68.1   **2.** 70.4   **3.** 12.1

4. 1.2   **5.** 33.3   **6.** 99.7

7. 885.6   **8.** 988.9   **9.** 601.5

0-7424-1815-4 *Numbers & Operations*

Answer Key

10. 1,000.08 **11.** 8.17 **12.** 40.44

13. 9.1 **14.** 220.81 **15.** 0.06

16. 60.81 **17.** 4,531.1 **18.** 66.01

19. 0.010 **20.** 1,111.011

21. 692.889 **22.** 7.012

23. 89.01 **24.** 5,001.045

25. 8.007 **26.** 200.779 **27.** 30.02

28–30. Answers will vary.

Fractions Are Percents, Too! 33

1. $\frac{1}{4}$, 0.25 **2.** 0.5, 50%

3. $\frac{1}{5}$, 0.2 **4.** $\frac{4}{10}$, 40%

5. $\frac{1}{2}$, 0.5 **6.** 0.4, 40%

A Quilt of Percents 34

24 yellow, 16 red, 24 green, 8 blue,
8 orange, 8 pink, 8 black, 4 purple

Household Appliances 35

Graph should be filled in to correctly
match percent given.

Decimals Are Fractions 36

1. 0.1 **2.** $\frac{2}{10} = \frac{1}{5}$

3. 0.3 **4.** $\frac{3}{10}$

5. $\frac{4}{10} = \frac{2}{5}$ **6.** $\frac{6}{10} = \frac{3}{5}$

7. 0.6 **8.** 0.4

Decimals Are Percentages, Too! . . 37

1. 40% **2.** 30%

3. 0.2 **4.** 30%

5. $\frac{5}{10} = \frac{1}{2}$ **6.** 80%

Decimals, Fractions, and Percents . . 38

1. 0.2, $\frac{2}{10}$, 20%

2. 0.4, $\frac{4}{10}$, 40%

3. 0.5, $\frac{5}{10}$, 50%

4. 0.05, $\frac{5}{100}$, 5%

5. 0.7, $\frac{7}{10}$, 70%

6. 0.09, $\frac{9}{100}$, 9%

7. 0.33, $\frac{1}{3}$, 33%

8. 0.01, $\frac{1}{100}$, 1%

9. 6 parts shaded

10. 1 part shaded

11. 7 parts shaded

12. 9.5 parts shaded

Do More: $\frac{3}{4} + \frac{1}{10} + \frac{7}{8} + \frac{95}{100}$

Fraction of an Area 39

1. C and D **2.** $\frac{1}{16}$

3. $\frac{7}{16}$ **4.** A

5. $\frac{7}{16} + \frac{4}{16} = \frac{11}{16}$

6. $\frac{4}{16} - \frac{1}{16} = \frac{3}{16}$

Do More: $6 \times B = 2\frac{10}{16} = 2\frac{5}{8}$;

$7 \times C = 1\frac{3}{4}$; $20 \times A = 1\frac{4}{16} = 1\frac{1}{4}$

Favorite Pie 40–41

Answers will vary.

Like Fractions 42

1. $\frac{2}{10} + \frac{1}{10} = \frac{3}{10}$

2. $\frac{4}{10} + \frac{3}{10} = \frac{7}{10}$

3. $\frac{4}{10} + \frac{2}{10} = \frac{6}{10} = \frac{3}{5}$

4. $\frac{4}{10} + \frac{2}{10} + \frac{1}{10} = \frac{7}{10}$

5. blue: 0.1, 10%

6. red: 0.2, 20%

7. purple: 0.3, 30%

8. yellow: 0.4, 40%

Comparing Unlike Fractions 43

1. $\frac{5}{6}$ **2.** $\frac{3}{8}$

3. $\frac{7}{8}$ **4.** $\frac{5}{8}$

5. $\frac{1}{3}$ **6.** $\frac{2}{3}$

7. $\frac{2}{4}$, $\frac{3}{6}$, $\frac{4}{8}$ (Answers may vary.)

8. $\frac{3}{9}$, $\frac{6}{18}$, $\frac{9}{27}$ (Answers may vary.)

Equivalent Fractions 44

1. $\frac{1}{2}$, $\frac{3}{6}$, $\frac{5}{10}$ **2.** $\frac{2}{6}$

3. $\frac{2}{8}$ **4.** $\frac{4}{6}$

5. $\frac{1}{2}$, $\frac{3}{6}$, $\frac{4}{8}$, $\frac{5}{10}$

6. $\frac{1}{2}$, $\frac{2}{4}$, $\frac{4}{8}$, $\frac{5}{10}$ **7.** $\frac{1}{3}$

8. $\frac{2}{3}$ **9.** $\frac{3}{4}$

10. $\frac{1}{2}$, $\frac{2}{4}$, $\frac{3}{6}$, $\frac{4}{8}$, $\frac{5}{10}$

11. > **12.** <

13. < **14.** >

Unlike Fractions 45

1. $\frac{1}{8} + \frac{2}{10} = \frac{5}{40} + \frac{8}{40} = \frac{13}{40}$

2. $\frac{2}{8} + \frac{4}{10} = \frac{10}{40} + \frac{16}{40} = \frac{26}{40} = \frac{13}{20}$

3. $\frac{3}{8} + \frac{3}{10} = \frac{15}{40} + \frac{12}{40} = \frac{27}{40}$

4. $\frac{2}{8} + \frac{1}{10} = \frac{10}{40} + \frac{4}{40} = \frac{14}{40} = \frac{7}{20}$

5. $\frac{1}{8} + \frac{2}{10} + \frac{2}{8} + \frac{4}{10} = \frac{6}{40} +$ $\frac{8}{40} + \frac{10}{40} + \frac{16}{40} = \frac{39}{40}$

6. $\frac{3}{8} + \frac{3}{10} + \frac{2}{8} = \frac{15}{40} + \frac{12}{40} + \frac{10}{40} = \frac{37}{40}$

Least Common Denominator 46

1. 15 **2.** 12 **3.** 14

4. 18 **5.** 12 **6.** 30

7. 10 **8.** 24 **9.** 30

10. $\frac{3}{6} + \frac{2}{6} = \frac{5}{6}$

11. $\frac{2}{8} - \frac{1}{8} = \frac{1}{8}$

12. $\frac{8}{10} - \frac{1}{10} = \frac{7}{10}$

13. $\frac{1}{12} + \frac{10}{12} = \frac{11}{12}$

Do More: There will be $\frac{1}{128}$ of the pie left.

 0-7424-1815-4 *Numbers & Operations*

Answer Key

Mixed Numbers 47

1. $\frac{13}{4}$ 2. $\frac{4}{3}$
3. $\frac{9}{2}$ 4. $\frac{21}{8}$
5. $\frac{11}{5}$ 6. $\frac{14}{3}$
7. $3\frac{1}{3}$ 8. $5\frac{1}{4}$
9. $6\frac{1}{2}$ 10. $3\frac{3}{5}$
11. $2\frac{1}{7}$ 12. $2\frac{1}{4}$

Number Line Fractions, Decimals, and Percents 48
Numbers correctly placed on number line.

1. 0.15, 25%, $\frac{1}{3}$, $\frac{6}{8}$
2. 10%, 66%, $\frac{7}{8}$, 0.9
3. $\frac{1}{5}$, 25%, $\frac{3}{10}$, 0.33
4. 0.2, 0.5, 70%, $\frac{8}{9}$
5. $\frac{1}{4}$, $\frac{5}{16}$, 40%, 0.8
6. 15%, 50%, 0.66, $\frac{7}{8}$

Least Common Multiple 49

1. 30 2. 20
3. 15 4. 30
5. 24 6. 21
7. 28 8. 15
9. 45 10. 36

Do More: They will meet after 36 minutes.

Finding Factors 50

1. **a.** the last digit is even
   b. the last digit is 5 or 0
   c. the last digit is 0
2. A number has a factor of 3 if the sum of its digits is a multiple of 3.
3. A number has a factor of 9 if the sum of ts digits is a multiple of 9.
4. **a.** 4 is a factor of: 128; 2,464; 272; 388; 2,300; 4,512.
   b. Yes, the trick always works (if you think of any number ending in 00 as being "100," which is divisible by 4.)

Do More: 6: A number has a factor of 6 if it has 2 AND 3 as factors (an even number whose digits have a sum that is a multiple of 3). 7: There is no trick for 7. 8: Any number that has a factor of 8 will also have a factor of 4. This helps eliminate many possibilities. If a number does not have a factor of 4, then it also won't have a factor of 8. If a number does have a factor of 4, then it must be tested to see if 8 is also a factor.

Positively Prime 51

1. 2 is the only even prime number. All other even numbers have a factor of 2.
2. Every prime number, except 2, is odd. But, not all odd numbers are prime. 9 is odd and has a factor of 3.
3. No. The product will automatically have 2 additional factors besides itself and 1.
4. The multiplication table shows many numbers that are not prime. If a number is found on the table (so long as it is not in the "1 x" row or column), then it is not prime.
5. **a–d.** no
   e. Answers may vary.
   f. $91 \div 13 = 7$
   g. No
6. 2, 3, 5, 7, 11, 13, 17, 19, 23, 29, 31, 41, 43, 47, 53, 59, 61, 67, 71, 73, 79, 83, and 97

Do More: Answers may vary. Students could use a 100-chart and cross out all multiples of the numbers 2–10. They could then test the remaining numbers to see if any have prime factors.

Greatest Common Factor 52

1. 10 2. 6
3. 5 4. 8
5. 4 6. 16

Check Your Skills—Number Systems . . 53

1. 4
2. 6
3. 10,800,056
4. 3,600,000
5. **a.** 8,000,000 + 900,000 + 70,000 + 6,000 + 400 + 20 + 4
   b. 70,000
6. 9
7. 10
8. 0.5, $\frac{1}{2}$, 50%; 0.01, $\frac{1}{100}$ 1%
9. $\frac{2}{4}$, $\frac{4}{8}$, $\frac{5}{10}$
10. $\frac{5}{8}$
11. 14
12. 30
13. 6
14. **a.** 4 squares shaded
    b. 60%
    c. $\frac{4}{10}$
    d. 0.4

Commutative Property of Addition . . 54

1. 312 2. 544
3. 344 4. 843
5. 183 6. 465
7. 913 8. 718

Associative Property of Addition . . 55

1–3. 175 4–7. Answers will vary.

It All Adds Up 56

1. $4 + 16 = 20$

0-7424-1815-4 Numbers & Operations

Answer Key

2. $(1 + 1) + 4 + 64 = 70$

3. $1 + (16 + 16) = 33$

4. $(4 + 4) + (16 + 16) = 40$

5. $(1 + 1 + 1) + (16 + 16) + 64 = 99$

6. $(1 + 1) + (64 + 64) = 130$

7. $(4 + 4) + 16 + 64 = 88$

8. $(1 + 1) + 16 = 18$

9. $4 + (16 + 16) = 36$

10. $(1 + 1 + 1) + (4 + 4 + 4) + (64 + 64 + 64) = 207$

11. $16 + (6 \times 64) = 400$

12. $(4 + 4 + 4) + (16 + 16) + (13 \times 64) = 876$

Do More: $(4 + 4) + (16 + 16) + (15 \times 64) = 1,000$

Matching Sums and Products 57

1. 25, e.   **2.** 28, a.

3. 40, f.   **4.** 42, b.

5. 45, c.   **6.** 56, d.

7. 48, j.   **8.** 35, g.

9. 20, h.   **10.** 32, i.

11. 30, o.   **12.** 72, n.

13. 24, m.   **14.** 63, k.

15. 36, l.

Do More: 27

Distance, Rate, and Time 58

1. a. 27 miles away

   b. multiplication

2. a. $27 \div 9 = 3$ hours

   b. yes

   c. time = distance ÷ rate

3. a. 8 mph

   b. division; rate = distance/time

Do More: The equations use opposite operations. They are inverses.

Commutative Property of Multiplication 59

1. a. $8 \times 4 = 32$

   b. $4 \times 8 = 32$

2. a. 15

   b. $5 \times 3 = 15$

   c. Students should draw 5 circles in each of the 3 boxes.

   d. $3 \times 5 = 15$

Do More: In each problem, the order of the numbers being multiplied was changed. This did not change the answers.

Distributive Property 60

1. a. $7 \times 11 = 77$

   b. $7 \times 8 + 7 \times 3 = 77$

   c. The answers are the same.

2. a. $5 \times 13 = 65$. Students should draw an area model with 5 rows and 13 columns.

   b. Answers will vary. One possible answer is $5 \times 10 + 5 \times 3$

   c. The answers are the same.

Multiplication Is the Opposite of Division 61

1. addition: $2 + 2 + 2 = 6, 3 + 3 = 6$

   multiplication: $2 \times 3 = 6, 3 \times 2 = 6$

   division: $6 \div 2 = 3, 6 \div 3 = 2$

2. addition: $3 + 3 + 3 + 3 = 12, 4 + 4 + 4 = 12$

   multiplication: $3 \times 4 = 12, 4 \times 3 = 12$

   division: $12 \div 3 = 4, 12 \div 4 = 3$

3. addition: $6 + 6 + 6 + 6 = 24, 4 + 4 + 4 + 4 + 4 + 4 = 24$

   multiplication: $6 \times 4 = 24, 4 \times 6 = 24$

   division: $24 \div 4 = 6, 24 \div 6 = 4$

4. addition: $4 + 4 + 4 + 4 + 4 = 20,$

$5 + 5 + 5 + 5 = 20$

   multiplication: $4 \times 5 = 20, 5 \times 4 = 20$

   division: $20 \div 4 = 5, 20 \div 5 = 4$

5. addition: $6 + 6 + 6 + 6 + 6 + 6 + 6 + 6 = 48, 8 + 8 + 8 + 8 + 8 + 8 = 48$

   multiplication: $6 \times 8 + 48, 8 \times 6 = 48$

   division: $48 \div 6 = 8, 48 \div 8 = 6$

Opposites 62

1. 80, 80   **2.** 30, 30

3. 48, 48   **4.** 18, 18

5. 12, 12   **6.** 32, 32

Division problems will vary for 7–22. One answer given.

7. $6 \times 9 = 54, 54 \div 6 = 9$

8. $4 \times 10 = 40, 40 \div 4 = 10$

9. $5 \times 7 = 35, 35 \div 5 = 7$

10. $8 \times 9 = 72, 72 \div 8 = 9$

11. $11 \times 9 = 99, 99 \div 11 = 9$

12. $6 \times 12 = 72, 72 \div 6 = 12$

13. $5 \times 9 = 45, 45 \div 5 = 9$

14. $3 \times 9 = 27, 27 \div 3 = 9$

15. $2 \times 9 = 18, 18 \div 2 = 9$

16. $4 \times 12 = 48, 48 \div 4 = 12$

17. $6 \times 7 = 42, 42 \div 6 = 7$

18. $11 \times 10 = 110, 110 \div 11 = 10$

19. $4 \times 9 = 36, 36 \div 4 = 9$

20. $7 \times 9 = 63, 63 \div 7 = 9$

21. $7 \times 4 = 28, 28 \div 7 = 4$

22. $2 \times 12 = 24, 24 \div 2 = 12$

Complete the Charts 63

1. 8, 2—10, 6, 16, 4

10, 5—15, 5, 50, 2

12, 4—16, 8, 48, 3

20, 2—22, 18, 40, 10

0-7424-1815-4 *Numbers & Operations*

Answer Key

50, 10—60, 40, 500, 5

2. 144, 6—150, 138, 864, 24

99, 3—102, 96, 297, 33

450, 18—468, 432, 8,100, 25

612, 4—616, 608, 2,448, 153

1,053, 13—1,066, 1,040, 13,689, 81

Do More: 0 and 1

Exploring Exponents 64

1. a. a, **b.** 9

2. a. b, **b.** 27

3. a. c, **b.** 81

Do More: 1 + 2 + 3 + 4 + 5 + 6 + 7 = 28 wishes

Down on the Farm 65

1. 5   **2.** 100

3. $\frac{1}{12}$ tablespoon   **4.** 10 weeks

5. 4 weeks   **6.** 192 bees

7. 2 weeks   **8.** 90 gallons

Do More: $374.97

Mable's Outfits 66

1. 9   **2.** 11

3. 8   **4.** 16

5. 8   **6.** 32

Eric's Sandwich Party 67

1. 4   **2.** 16

3. 8   **4.** 60

5. 4   **6.** 20

Biscuit Pizzas 68

1. $1.86

2. 1 $\frac{1}{2}$ pounds

3. 6 cups

4. 6:40 P.M.

5. 3 cups

Multiplication Table 69

Table should be filled in correctly.

Checking the Facts 70

1. 4 + 1 = 5   **2.** 2 + 8 = 16

4 x 1 = 4   2 x 8 = 16

4 ÷ 1 = 4   8 ÷ 2 = 4

3. 4 + 8 = 12   **4.** 3 + 9 = 12

4 x 8 = 32   3 x 9 = 27

8 ÷ 4 = 2   9 ÷ 3 = 3

5. 5 + 10 = 15   **6.** 2 + 10 = 12

5 x 10 = 50   2 x 10 = 20

10 ÷ 5 = 2   10 ÷ 2 = 5

7. 3 + 12 = 15   **8.** 3 + 15 = 18

3 x 12 = 36   3 x 15 = 45

12 ÷ 3 = 4   15 ÷ 3 = 5

9. 6 + 12 = 18   **10.** 5 + 15 = 20

6 x 12 = 72   5 x 15 = 75

12 ÷ 6 = 2   15 ÷ 5 = 3

Finding Multiplication Facts 71

Answers will vary.

The Sum of It All 72

55   155

255   355

455   555

655   755

855   955

Grand Total: 5,050

Do More: 1 + 99 = 100, 2 + 98 = 100, etc. 50 sets of 100 plus the 50 left in the middle makes 5,050.

Multiplying Mice 73

January = 2

February = 8

March = 32

April = 128

May = 384 + 128 = 512

June = 1,536 + 512 = 2,048

July = 6,144 + 2,048 = 8,192

August = 24,576 + 8,192 = 32,768

September = 98,304 + 32,768 = 131,072

October = 393,216 + 131,072 = 524,288

November = 1,572,864 + 524,288 = 2,097,152

December = 6,291,456 + 2,097,152 = 8,388,608

1. more   **2.** November

3. 8,000   **4.** 8,388,608

Daily Double 74

1. $0.01   **2.** $0.02

3. $0.04   **4.** $0.08

5. $0.16   **6.** $0.32

7. $0.64   **8.** $1.28

9. $2.56   **10.** $5.12

11. $10.24   **12.** $20.48

13. $40.96   **14.** $81.92

15. $163.84   **16.** $327.68

17. $655.36   **18.** $1,310.72

19. $2,621.44   **20.** $5,242.88

21. $10,485.76   **22.** $20,971.52

23. $41,943.04   **24.** $83,886.08

25. $167,772.16 **26.** $335,544.32

27. $671,088.64 **28.** $1,342,177.28

0-7424-1815-4 *Numbers & Operations*

Answer Key

Daily Double 75

1–2. Answers will vary.

3. day 15   **4.** $1.27

5. $2,348,810.24

6. $2,684,354.56

7. 21   **8.** 19 and 20

9. 28th   **10.** $162.56

Check Your Skills—Operations . . . 76

1. sum   **2.** grouped

3. multiplied   **4.** 3 and 4

5. order, factors   **6.** $9 \times 5 = 45$

7. $4 + 4 + 4 + 4 + 4 + 4 = 24$, $4 \times 6 = 24$, $24 \div 6 = 4$ (Answers may vary.)

8. 3^2

9. 2 weeks, multiplication

10. Students should correctly list 8 times table facts.

A Quick Way to Solve Problems . 77

1. 80,000,000   **2.** 500,000

3. 5,000,000   **4.** 60,000,000

5. 11,000,000   **6.** 3,200,000,000

7. 890,000,000   **8.** 5,500,000

9. 500,000   **10.** 10,000

Adding Decimals 78

1. 661.01   **2.** 363.19

3. 35.73   **4.** 49.89

5. 279.17   **6.** 204.76

7. 197.33   **8.** 1,560.01

The Fundraiser 79

1. $1,019.55   **2.** $243.47

3. $1,239.57   **4.** $996.10

5. $45.27

Do More: $16,910.16

Subtracting Decimals 80

1. 45.87   **2.** 88.099

3. 1.479   **4.** 854.554

5. Yes, he has $6.06 left.

6. $16.55

7. $4.25

Sums and Differences of Like Fractions 81

1. $\frac{2}{2} = 1$ **2.** $\frac{3}{4}$

3. $\frac{2}{5}$ **4.** $\frac{3}{6} = \frac{1}{2}$

5. $\frac{4}{5}$ **6.** $\frac{4}{6} = \frac{2}{3}$

7. $\frac{1}{4}$ **8.** $\frac{4}{8} = \frac{1}{2}$

9. $\frac{8}{8} = 1$ **10.** $\frac{2}{3}$

Simplifying Improper Fractions . . 82

1. 2 oranges

2. $2\frac{2}{3}$ oranges

3. $\frac{14}{12} = 1\frac{2}{12} = 1\frac{1}{6}$

4. $\frac{18}{12} = 1\frac{6}{12} = 1\frac{1}{2}$

5. $\frac{16}{12} = 1\frac{4}{12} = 1\frac{1}{3}$

6. $\frac{20}{12} = 1\frac{8}{12} = 1\frac{2}{3}$

Mixed Number Sums 83

1. $\frac{26}{12} = 2\frac{2}{12} = 2\frac{1}{6}$

2. **a.** 26

 b. $26 \div 12 = 2 \text{ R2}$, $2\frac{2}{12} = 2\frac{1}{6}$

3. $\frac{4}{2} = 2$

4. $\frac{6}{4} = 1\frac{2}{4} = 1\frac{1}{2}$

5. $\frac{7}{6} = 1\frac{1}{6}$

6. $\frac{12}{8} = 1\frac{4}{8} = 1\frac{1}{2}$

7. $\frac{6}{3} = 2$

8. $\frac{9}{6} = 1\frac{3}{6} = 1\frac{1}{2}$

9. $\frac{7}{5} = 1\frac{2}{5}$

10. $\frac{16}{12} = 1\frac{4}{12} = 1\frac{1}{3}$

Subtracting Unlike Fractions 84

1. $\frac{1}{4} - \frac{1}{6} = \frac{3}{12} - \frac{2}{12} = \frac{1}{12}$

2. $\frac{1}{6} - \frac{1}{12} = \frac{2}{12} - \frac{1}{12} = \frac{1}{12}$

3. $\frac{1}{8} - \frac{1}{12} = \frac{3}{24} - \frac{2}{24} = \frac{1}{24}$

4. $\frac{1}{4} - \frac{1}{12} = \frac{3}{12} - \frac{1}{12} = \frac{2}{12} = \frac{1}{6}$

5. $\frac{1}{4} - \frac{1}{8} = \frac{2}{8} - \frac{1}{8} = \frac{1}{8}$

Do More: When you multiply by a fraction.

Adding and Subtracting Unlike Fractions 85

1. $\frac{3}{12} + \frac{6}{12} = \frac{9}{12} = \frac{3}{4}$

2. $\frac{9}{18} - \frac{8}{18} = \frac{1}{18}$

3. $\frac{24}{30} + \frac{5}{30} = \frac{29}{30}$

4. $\frac{1}{10} + 1 = 1\frac{1}{10}$

5. $\frac{14}{21} + \frac{9}{21} = \frac{23}{21} = 1\frac{2}{21}$

6. $\frac{9}{12} - \frac{4}{12} = \frac{5}{12}$

7. $\frac{8}{24} + \frac{9}{24} = \frac{17}{24}$

8. $\frac{1}{7} + 1 = 1\frac{1}{7}$

9. $\frac{24}{30} + \frac{5}{30} = \frac{29}{30}$

10. $\frac{5}{10} + \frac{4}{10} = \frac{9}{10}$

Fraction Subtraction 86

1. $\frac{3}{6} - \frac{2}{6} = \frac{1}{6}$

2. $\frac{2}{8} - \frac{1}{8} = \frac{1}{8}$

3. $\frac{2}{6} - \frac{1}{6} = \frac{1}{6}$

4. $\frac{4}{12} - \frac{3}{12} = \frac{1}{12}$

5. $\frac{2}{4} - \frac{1}{4} = \frac{1}{4}$

6. $\frac{4}{8} - \frac{1}{8} = \frac{3}{8}$

7. $\frac{6}{15} - \frac{5}{15} = \frac{1}{15}$

8. $\frac{6}{8} - \frac{3}{8} = \frac{3}{8}$

9. $\frac{1}{6}$ to Leon; Stan ate $\frac{2}{6}$ or $\frac{1}{3}$ of a sandwich

0-7424-1815-4 *Numbers & Operations*

Answer Key

10. $\frac{1}{4} \times \frac{1}{2} = \frac{1}{8}$, $\frac{1}{4} - \frac{1}{8} = \frac{1}{8}$

11. $1.50

12. $\frac{1}{2} \times \frac{1}{4} = \frac{1}{8}$, $\frac{1}{2} + \frac{1}{8} = \frac{5}{8}$, $1 - \frac{5}{8} = \frac{3}{8}$

Multiplying Fractions 87

1. $\frac{4}{10} = \frac{2}{5}$ 2. $\frac{4}{20} = \frac{1}{5}$
3. $\frac{3}{12} = \frac{1}{4}$ 4. $\frac{5}{30} = \frac{1}{6}$
5. $\frac{3}{15} = \frac{1}{5}$ 6. $\frac{12}{24} = \frac{1}{2}$
7. $\frac{3}{36} = \frac{1}{12}$ 8. $\frac{4}{40} = \frac{1}{10}$
9. $\frac{4}{14} = \frac{2}{7}$ 10. $\frac{6}{48} = \frac{1}{8}$

Dividing Fractions 88

1. $\frac{4}{3} = 1\frac{1}{3}$ 2. $\frac{3}{4}$
3. $\frac{8}{20} = \frac{2}{5}$ 4. $\frac{5}{12}$
5. $\frac{4}{3} = 1\frac{1}{3}$ 6. $\frac{4}{4} = 1$
7. $\frac{8}{30} = \frac{4}{15}$ 8. $\frac{21}{5} = 4\frac{1}{5}$
9. $\frac{3}{25}$ 10. $\frac{6}{25}$
11. $\frac{2}{40} = \frac{1}{20}$ 12. $\frac{1}{64}$

Adding and Subtracting Integers . . 89

1. ⁻3   2. ⁺6
3. ⁻4   4. ⁻7
5. ⁻6   6. ⁻14
7. 0   8. ⁻3
9. ⁻6   10. ⁻13
11. ⁻2   12. ⁺9

Multiplying Integers 90

1. ⁻15   2. ⁺56
3. ⁻500   4. ⁺2,151
5. ⁺10,506   6. ⁻72,720
7. ⁻18,349   8. ⁺63.04
9. ⁻510.12   10. ⁺427.5

Dividing Integers 91

1. ⁻50   2. ⁻11

3. ⁻31 R4   4. ⁺159
5. ⁻20   6. ⁻8
7. ⁻191   8. ⁺202
9. ⁻213   10. ⁺33

Climbing the Multiplication Pyramid . . 92

bottom row: 0, 1, 2, 3, 4, 5

row 2: 0, 2, 6, 12, 20

row 3: 0, 12, 72, 240

row 4: 0, 864, 17,280

row 5: 0, 14,929,920

top row: 0

Long Division Practice 93

1. 13 R5   2. 45
3. 57   4. 10 R29
5. 22 R25   6. 14 R27
7. 11 R42   8. 11 R57
9. 19   10. 19 R20
11. 11 R8   12. 13 R46

Magic Pizza 94

1. $\frac{1}{4} + \frac{1}{4} = \frac{2}{4} \times \frac{3}{1} = \frac{6}{4} = 1\frac{1}{2}$ cups

2. $\frac{1}{2} \times \frac{4}{1} = \frac{4}{2} = 2$ cups

3. $2T + 2T = 4T \times 24 = 96T$, $\frac{96}{16} = 6$ cups Parmesan; 1 cup $\times 24 = 24$ cups mozzarella

4. 2 cups per pizza = 40 cups

Magic Pizzas 95

1. 25%

2. $\frac{1}{2} \times 12 = 6$ cups

3. $\frac{2}{10}$ = milk, $\frac{1}{10}$ = biscuit mix, $\frac{1}{10}$ = Parmesan cheese, $\frac{2}{10}$ = mozzarella cheese, $\frac{1}{20}$ pepper, $\frac{1}{20}$ onions, $\frac{2}{10}$ beef, $\frac{1}{10}$ sauce

Ratio 96

1. 9:10   2. 4:5
3. 2:5 and 2:7   4. equivalent
5. equivalent   6. not equivalent
7. 3:1   8. 8:32
9. 45:50

Percents and Ratios 97

1. 1   2. 3
3. 9:10   4. 10
5. 0   6. 1:10

Do More: $\frac{1}{2} + \frac{1}{3} = \frac{3}{6} + \frac{2}{6} = \frac{5}{6}$
$1 - \frac{5}{6} = \frac{1}{6}$

Percents, Fractions, and Decimals . . . 98

1. 30%, $\frac{7}{10}$, 0.3
2. 90%, $\frac{9}{10}$, 0.1
3. 50%, $\frac{5}{10}$, 0.5
4. 25%, $\frac{1}{4}$, 0.75
5. 30%, $\frac{7}{10}$, 0.7
6. 100%, 0, 1.0
7. 95%, $\frac{5}{10}$, 0.5
8. 10%, $\frac{9}{10}$, 0.5

Counting Household Appliances . . 99

1. 98   2. 420
3. 135   4. 10
5. 5   6. 970
7. 225   8. 770

Is It Enough? 100

1. 80%
2. 0.80 x 112 = $89.60
3. $78.40 (30% off = 70% of the regular price; 0.70 x 112 = 78.4)
4. a. 0.04 x 78.4 = $3.14 tax
b. Yes. $78.4 + $3.14 = $81.54. She has $85.
5. $18.40 (30% off = 70% of the

Published by Instructional Fair. Copyright protected.   0-7424-1815-4 *Numbers & Operations*

Answer Key

regular price; 0.70 x 112 = 78.4; cost is $78.40 − $60 = $18.40)

6. **a.** $95.20 (15% off = 85% of the regular price; 0.85 x 112 = 95.2)

   b. $3.81 (0.04 x 95.2 = 3.81)

Do More: If it is 25% off, that means the sale price is 75% of the regular price. Multiply 0.75 by the regular price.

Papa's Burger Barn 101

1. $8.04
2. $16.50
3. $6.75
4. $7.50
5. $9.00
6. $9.64

Estimating Percentages 102

1. $23.40
2. $540
3. $885.09
4. $44; $594 $3,885.09

Interest 103

1. $6,000 \times 0.06 \times \frac{1}{2}$ year = $180; $180 + 6,000 = $6,180
2. $500 \times 0.03 \times 1$ year = $15; $15 + 500 = $515
3. $1,000 \times 0.1 \times \frac{1}{4}$ year (0.25) = 25; 1,000 + 25 = $1,025
4. $10,000 \times 0.05 \times 2 = 1,000$, 10,000 + 1,000 = $11,000
5. $2,500 \times 0.10 \times 20 = 5,000$ 2,500 + 5,000 = $7,500

Estimating Products 104

1. 19,533
2. 32,670
3. 44,252
4. 90,870
5. 50,904
6. 38,112
7. 30,086
8. 146,376
9. 18,753
10. 37,766

Estimating Quotients 105

1. 84
2. 45
3. 36
4. 99
5. 93
6. 55
7. 89
8. 102

---

9. 87
10. 85

Parking Problems 106

1. **a.** 600 cars (2,400 ÷ 4 = 600)
   b. 1,200 motorcycles (2,400 ÷ 2 = 1,200)
   c. 133 18-wheelers (2,400 ÷ 18 = 133 R6)
2. 100 motorcycles ($\frac{1}{12}$ x 2,400 = 200 wheels; 200 wheels ÷ 2 wheels per motorcycle = 100 motorcycles)
3. 72 tires on 18-wheelers (4 x 18 = 72 tires)
4. **a.** 532 4-wheel vehicles (2,400 − 200 − 72 = 2,128 tires; 2,128 tires ÷ 4 tires per vehicle = 532 vehicles)
   b. 133 minivans (532 x $\frac{1}{4}$ = 133)
   c. 266 cars (532 x $\frac{1}{2}$ = 266)

Missing Numbers 107

1. 5
2. 100
3. 4
4. 90
5. 12
6. triangle = 5
7. hexagon = 6
8. trapezoid = 4

Check Your Skills—Computation . 108

1. 38.23
2. 854.554
3. $1\frac{1}{2}$
4. $\frac{5}{12}$
5. $\frac{5}{30} = \frac{1}{6}$
6. $\frac{3}{4}$
7. ⁻17
8. ⁺2
9. 4,275
10. ⁻98
11. $\frac{24}{2} = 12$
12. 25:100, or 1:4
13. 0.25
14. $\frac{3}{12}$, or $\frac{1}{4}$
15. 0.66
16. 7 squares shaded
    a. 30%
    b. $\frac{3}{10}$
    c. 0.3

Post Test 109–110

1. 9
2. 789,403
3. 67,000
4. **a.** 8,000,000 + 10,000 + 2
   b. 10,000
5. 3
6. 0.75, $\frac{3}{4}$, 75%
7. 0.1, $\frac{1}{10}$, 10%
8. 40
9. 6
10. Changing the order of the addends does not change the sum.
11. Changing the grouping of the addends does not change the sum.
12. dividend, divisor, quotient
13. commutative property
14. 8 + 8 + 8 + 8 = 32
15. 5 + 5 + 5 + 5 + 5 = 25, 5 x 5 = 25, 25 ÷ 5 = 5
16. 3^2
17. 1 week
18. $\frac{12}{4}$ = 3 cups of butter
19. 81.25
20. 965.3
21. $\frac{4}{8} = \frac{1}{2}$
22. $\frac{3}{12} = \frac{1}{4}$
23. $\frac{4}{20} = \frac{1}{5}$
24. $\frac{4}{8} = \frac{1}{2}$
25. ⁻3
26. 10,857
27. ⁻513
28. 145
29. 36
30. 25, 20: 45, 5, 500, 1.25 100, 5: 105, 95, 500, 20 1,000, 10: 1,010, 990, 10,000,100

 0-7424-1815-4 *Numbers & Operations*

associative property of addition	associative property of multiplication
common denominator	commutative property of addition
decimal	denominator

0-7424-1815-4 *Numbers & Operations*

The way factors are grouped does not change the product.

$$(1 \times 7) \times 8 = 1 \times (7 \times 8)$$

The way addends are grouped does not change the sum.

$$3 + (4 + 1) = (3 + 4) + 1$$

The order of the addends does not change the sum.

$$3 + 4 = 4 + 3$$

When renaming fractions so that they have the same denominator, the smallest number that each can be divided into is the common denominator. 12 is the common denominator for $\frac{1}{3}$ and $\frac{1}{4}$.

The number below the fraction bar in a fraction.
$$\frac{1}{3}$$

A number with one or more digits to the right of a decimal point.
2.34 and 0.02 are decimals.

0-7424-1815-4 *Numbers & Operations*

equivalent fractions	factors
fraction	hundredth
improper fraction	integers

The numbers that are multiplied to get a product.

Example: $3 \times 4 = 12$

Fractions that name the same number are equivalent.
Example:

$$\frac{2}{4} = \frac{1}{2}$$

One of one hundred equal parts of a whole. Examples:

$$\frac{1}{100} \text{ or } 1\% \text{ or } 0.01$$

are all ways to express one hundredth.

A number that names part of a whole or part of a set.

Example: $\dfrac{1}{2}$

All positive and negative whole numbers.

A fraction in which the numerator is greater than or equal to the denominator. Example: $\dfrac{6}{5}$ is an improper fraction because it could be broken down and written 1 and $\dfrac{1}{5}$

least common denominator

mixed number

multiples

negative integers

numerator

percent

0-7424-1815-4 *Numbers & Operations*

A number written as a whole number and a fraction.

Example: $3\frac{1}{3}$

The least common multiple of the denominators of two or more fractions.

Example:

For $\frac{1}{3}$ and $\frac{1}{4}$,

12 is the least common denominator.

An integer with a value less than zero. On a number line, negative integers are on the left side of 0.

Examples: $-3, -1$

The products of one given number and all other whole number. Example: 8 and 12 are multiples of 4.

A special ratio that compares a number with one hundred. Example: 25% = 25 out of 100

The number above the fraction bar in a fraction. Example:

$\frac{2}{5}$

0-7424-1815-4 *Numbers & Operations*

positive integers

ratio

reciprocals

simplest form

tenth

thousandth

0-7424-1815-4 *Numbers & Operations*

The comparison of 2 quantities is a ratio. Example: 2 people out of 5 people is 2:5.

An integer greater than 0. On a number line, positive integers are on the right side of zero. Examples: +1, +3

A fraction is in simplest form when the greatest common factor of the numerator and denominator is 1.

Example:

$\dfrac{1}{3}$ and $\dfrac{1}{7}$

Two fractions whose product is 1 are reciprocal.

Example: $\dfrac{3}{5} \times \dfrac{5}{3} = 1$

One of one thousand equal parts of a whole is a thousandth.

Examples: $\dfrac{1}{1,000}$; 0.1%;

1:1,000; or 0.001

One of ten equal parts of a whole is a tenth.

Examples: $\dfrac{1}{10}$, 10%,

1:10, or 0.1

0-7424-1815-4 *Numbers & Operations*